R. Atkinson Fox

William M. Thompson

Robert Atkinson Fox
(1860-1935)

R. Atkinson Fox

William M. Thompson

IDENTIFICATION & PRICE GUIDE

by

Patricia L. Gibson

Collectors Press
Portland, Oregon

DISCLAIMER

The vast information in this book has been compiled from the most reliable sources. Sincere efforts have been made to eliminate errors and questionable information. Nevertheless, errors are possible in a work of this scope. Neither the publisher nor the author will be held responsible for losses that may occur in either the purchase, sale or any other type of transaction because of information contained herein.

Copyright © 1995 Collectors Press

All rights reserved. No part of this book may be reproduced or transmitted in any form or by any means, electronic or mechanical, including photocopying, recording, or by any information storage and retrieval system, without permission in writing from the publisher.

Photograph of R.A. Fox courtesy Rick & Charlotte Martin

A varying number of images contained herein were originally published by Brown & Bigelow, Inc.

First Edition, 1995

Printed in the United States of America
54321

ISBN 0-9635202-1-0 : $19.95
Library of Congress CCN : 94-070639

Additional copies of this book may be purchased by sending $19.95 plus $2.50 shipping to:

Collectors Press
P.O. Box 230986
Portland, OR 97281

VISA/MasterCard call (503) 684-3030

Contents

Acknowledgments 8
Introduction 9
Market Review 11

R. Atkinson Fox
    Portraits 15
    Enchanted Girls 19
    Lady Riders 25
    Mothers & Children 31
    Dogs 37
    Horses 44
    Cows 51
    Feline Family & Bears 66
    Animals - Variety 70
    Gardens 80
    Cottages & Rural Landscapes 89
    Rivers & Falls 98
    Mountains & Lakes 111
    Roads & Pathways 128
    Ships & Seascapes 135
    Hunting & Fishing 141
    Western 144
    Native Americans 147
    Military & Presidents 151
    Planes & Trains & Miscellaneous 156

Fox Pseudonyms
    Introduction 163
    L. H. Banks 165
    G. Blanchard Carr 166

J. Colvin 167
DeForest 170
Dupre 175
Elmer Louis 177
Musson 182
George W. Turner 183
Wainright 170
George White 190
G. Wood 193

William M. Thompson 195
   Moonlight 197
   Rural Landscapes 202
   Mountains & Other Landscapes 208
   Rivers & Falls 214
   Campfires 219
   Cottages & Gardens 222
   Snow Scenes 226
   Ships & Sea 238

Index 241

Dedicated to my family and friends
and all of the Fox collectors who
have helped me add to my collection

Acknowledgments

There are many friends, collectors and family members I would like to thank for their help and support in making this book possible and for helping me add to my collection over the years.

Thanks go to Rita Mortenson who made the initial contact with the Fox family and started the Fox Hunt Newsletter that I always enjoy receiving. Without Rita's work, R.A. Fox may have never been so widely popular.

I would also like to thank the R.A. Fox Society and its members who continue to offer new information about Fox at their annual convention.

Many thanks to my two kids Thomas and Sherry for tolerating my sometimes frenzied collecting habits, my cousins Billy and Buck for their moral support and Laurelwood Antiques in San Jose, California for giving me the ongoing encouragement to keep my collection growing.

Finally, I would like to thank the publisher, Richard Perry, for convincing me of the need for this book. Also his photographer Sid Smith and Phil and Sue Jaegeling for their help during the long photographic sessions. Without Richard, this much needed book would never have happened. I owe him a great deal of gratitude for his confidence in me.

R. A. Fox Introduction

R. Atkinson Fox was a prolific illustrator of calendars, posters, postcards, picture puzzles, and advertising materials from the late 1900s until about 1930. Brown & Bigelow, a major publishing firm, once noted that more reproductions had been made of Fox's work's than of the works of any other living artist.

Although Fox painted whatever subjects publishers requested -- including, in the 1920s, those typical of the Art Deco mode--his strength was naturalism. A painter of mainly landscapes, portraits, and rural subjects, he was especially admired for his horses, cows, and mountains. Although some of his work has been by beginning collectors confused with that of Maxfield Parrish, he was not, like Parrish, a photographic realist. His technique was softer and warmer, allowing more room for imaginative interpretation.

Fox was a professional painter before he turned illustrator. Although little information has been uncovered about his early life, we know that he took up art at an early age. Born in Toronto, Ontario, on December 11, 1860, Fox was the son of a Presbyterian minister. Fox left home in his mid teens, apparently to further his study of art. For four years he studied art with John Wesley Bridgman, a portrait painter and member of the Ontario Society of Artists.

From the age of seventeen to about the age of twenty-four, Fox made his living primarily as a portrait artist. He painted the portraits of such notables as President Grover Cleveland, President Benjamin Harrison, Sir John MacDonald, and Princess Louise of England. His paintings were exhibited at both the Ontario Society of Artists and the Royal Canadian Academy of Arts. Also, at some point in his twenties, he studied art and traveled extensively in Europe. Some speculate that he was influenced by the Barbizon School of painters in Paris. Like them, Fox used lighting and muted colors to create a mood of gentle, natural beauty.

In the late 1880s, Fox moved to New York City. In the 1890s, his paintings were auctioned in New York and Boston, exhibited with the Art Club of Philadelphia and the New York Academy.

At the turn of the century, Fox moved to Philadelphia, where he married a concert pianist; we don't know when they wed, or even her name, for he didn't discuss this marriage with his later family and friends. His first wife died in 1901.

In 1903 Fox married Anna Marie Gaffney, who was born in Salem, Massachusetts, to Irish immigrants. Anna was twenty-five at the time of the marriage; Fox was almost forty-three. Their early years together were marked by frequent moves and frequent births. From 1904 to 1920, Anna gave birth to eight children, all of whom survived into adulthood. During these years, the family lived in New Jersey--mostly in towns near Philadelphia, where most of Fox's business was at the time. They moved several more times before settling on a farm in West Long Branch, New Jersey. The moves were apparently prompted not only by the family's growing number, but also by its growing fortune, as Fox expanded his clientele among calendar, printing, and picture-frame companies.

From West Long Branch, Fox made frequent trips to Chicago, the home of a major client, the John Baumgarth Company (which was later sold to Brown & Bigelow). After Fox was hit by an automobile in Chicago on one of his business trips, the family decided to move to Chicago so Fox wouldn't have to travel so far.

In Chicago, the family moved several times, each time to a bigger house. Fox rented several studios in succession, almost all within walking distance of home.

Fox was a tireless worker. He painted in his studio every day, from memory, from sketches, and from photographs (he had never been to the West when he painted his Western landscapes). He often completed a painting in a day. Afterward, he would patiently make alterations to his paintings that were requested by the publisher. Reproductions of over a thousand of Fox's paintings have been identified, and prints of others are sure to be found.

Because late in his career Fox painted almost exclusively on commission for publication, he didn't always intend these painting to last. Nor was he always pleased with his work as evidenced by his frequent use of pseudonyms.

After several years of ill health, Fox died in 1935 of heart disease and arteriosclerosis, which were complicated by bronchitis. His wife, Anna, remained in good health until her death twenty-nine years later.

R. Atkinson Fox's prints have been popular among collectors for decades. Little was known about the man, however, before 1980, when Rita Mortenson, an antique dealer, placed an ad in The Antique Trader pleading for information. Now "Fox hunters," as they call themselves, hold an annual convention, and interest in Fox's work continues to grow.

Market Review

The paintings of R.A. Fox were reproduced for both calendar and print markets. The vast numbers of varying image sizes ranging from as small as 1.5 by 2.5 inches up to 20 inches by 40 inches, were made for a variety of different markets.

The sizes indicated in this guide have all been verified, but it is possible that you may encounter a piece that varies from the size that is listed. Further, it is not uncommon to find a Fox that has been cropped or portioned, as Fox collectors like to call it. This is because often times calendar companies would cut an image to fit one of their stock calendar blanks. When reproduced in another size for instance, one could encounter the entire image. Because of the flexibility of print and framing companies, they were more likely to use the entire image by customizing the frame to the image, as opposed to large calendar companies who commonly customized the image to the frame. The underlying factors in determining value are size, condition and scarcity. In determining the value of a Fox calendar as opposed to just the image, one can typically add $25 for the calendar.

Damage to a piece in the form of color fading, stains, small and large tears etc., affects value and will significantly lower the prices listed in this book. If, however, the piece is scarce, price may not fluctuate as greatly as it would with the more common pieces. Most collectors believe it is better to collect something hard to find in poor condition than to not own the piece at all.

The original frame adds value to a piece, especially when it's particularly attractive and in good condition. The paper backing behind a print does not affect the value of a Fox, unlike other artists who's works are commonly reproduced even today. Because so few new reproductions exist, it is highly unlikely that what you find framed or unframed is new. Buying from a reputable dealer, however, can almost guarantee that what you buy is original.

New reproductions of Fox's works have not yet been found to any significant degree. Of course, laser copies can be made in virtually any size, but they are easily identified by the shiny paper used, the over exaggerated color and the poor clarity of the image.

Following is the only six Fox reproductions known to have been legitimately reproduced.

1. The Right of Way. 22 X 17.5 (1986)
2. An Old Fashioned Garden. 22 X 16 (1988)
3. Sunrise. 20 X 16 (1989)
4. Giant Steps Falls. 12 X 9 (1989)
5. Where Brooks Send Up a Cheerful Tune. 20 X 16 (1989)
6. June Morn. 20 X 16 (1993)

R. ATKINSON FOX

Portraits 15

Glory of Youth. 20×16, $350. 8×6, $150.

Meditation #1. 11×8, $275.

Roses Fair. 13×10, $285. 9.5×7, $195.

Fascinating. 11×8, $275.

16 *Portraits*

A Fair Guide. 20×16, $325. 10×8, $195.   Water Lilies. 4×6, $195. 3×5, $175.

The Village Belle. 22×28, $375.   Chrysanthemums. 8×6, $295.

Maud Muller. *Postcard,* $125.

A Fair Skipper. 9×4.5, $195.

Mid Flowers Fair. 8×6, $250. 5.5×4, $195.

Beauties of the Country. 12×8.5, $165. *Postcard,* $85.

18 *Portraits*

Pride of the Farm #1. 11.5×9, $225.

The Best Piemaker in Town. 5.5×7.5, $250.

The Prize Winner. 11×9, $225. 9×6, $195.

Carefree. 9×11, $225. *Fan*, $150.

Enchanted Girls

Elysian Fields. 16×20, $150. 10×13, $135. 10×12, $100. 4×5, $75. *Thermometer,* $85.

Oriental Dreams. 16×20, $125. 9×12, $95.

Day Dreams #1. 11×14, $250. 7.5×11 $195. 5×7, $125. *Puzzle,* $85.

Dawn. 18×30, $275. 10×18, $125. 9×15, $95.

Sunset Dreams. 18×30, $275. 10×18, $125. 9×15, $95.

In the Valley of Enchantment. 22×27, $275. 18×22, $225. 9×12, $145. 7×9, $125.

20 *Enchanted Girls*

Daydreams #2. 16×20, $150. 10×12, $100. 4×5, $85. *Greeting Card*, $75.

Love's Paradise. 18×30, $275. 10×18, $125. 9×15, $95.

The Valley of Enchantment #1. 9×12, $175. 6×8, $125. *Puzzle*, $85.

Twilight. 12×16, $165.

My Castle of Dreams. 9×12, $225. 9×14, $195. 7×9, $165. 4.5×7.75, $125. *Thermometer,* $135.

Spirit of Youth. 18×30, $275. 10×18, $125. 9×15, $95.

Enchanted Girls 21

Meditation #2. 8.5×6.5, $195.

Music of the Waters. 20×16, $150. 12×9, $100. 8×6, $85. 5.5×3.75, $75. *Thermometer,* $75. *Puzzle,* $75. *Wood Plaque,* $55.

The Valley of Enchantment #2. 13×10, $175. 10.5×8.5, $150. 10×5, $85.

Sunrise #1. 20×16, $165. 16×12, $135. 12×10, $125. 8×6, $95. 5×4, $85. 2.5×4, $65. *Metal Box,* $95. *Thermometer,* $85. *Fan,* $75. *Ink Blotter,* $65.

22 *Enchanted Girls*

The Gates of Dreamland. 14×10.5, $225. 8×5.5, $175.

Romance Canyon. 18×12, $165. 15×12, $145. 8×6, $85. 3.5×3.75, $65. *Puzzle*, $85. *Thermometer*, $85. *Wood Box*, $85. *Ink Blotter*, $55.

Dream Castle. 12×10, $200. 10×8, $150.

June Morn. 20×13, $200. 18×14.5, $185.

Spirit of the Harvest. 8×6, $250.

Oriental Beauties. 8×10, $285. 5×7, $250.

Cleopatra. 7×9, $285.

The Adventuress. 5×3.75, $185.

In My Garden of Dreams. 23×10, $225.
13×10, $165. 10×8, $125. 8×6, $95.

Lady Riders

Deering. 20.5×13.5, $275. 14×11, $250. 13×12, $200.

Jealousy. 16×12, $225. 11.5×8.5, $175.

Faithful and True #2. 8×6, $175.

O.... . 15×9, $250.

26 Lady Riders

The Treat. 7×5, $250.

Old Pals. 9×7, $200. 6×4, $150.

Her Pet. 12×9, $175. 8×6, $150.

Ready for a Cantor. 11×8, $225.

Lady Riders 27

Friends #1. 12×9, $225.

Bluegrass Beauties. 9×7, $185. *Fan*, $125.

Untitled #3. 12×8, $225.

Untitled #6. 6×4, $195.

Lady Riders

A Treat. 9×12, $250. 8×11, $225.

Untitled #9. 9×7, $225.

Thoroughbreds #1. 12×8, $175. 5×4, $150. *Both 1921 Almanac Covers.*

Fooling Him. 6×8, $195.

Lady Riders 29

My Pet. 9.25×6.75, $200.

In the North Woods. 10×8, $225. 8×6, $200.

The Girl of the Golden West #1. 9×6 oval, $275.

Three Friends. 11×8, $275.

The Girl of the Golden West #2. 16×12, $200. 12×10, $185. *Puzzle*, $125.

Mothers & Children 31

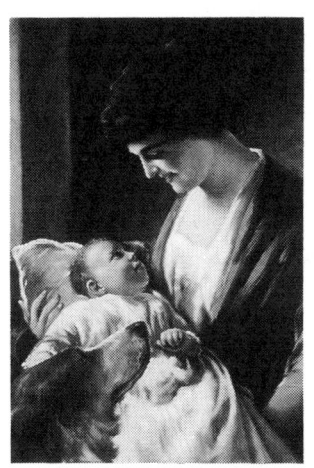

Look Pretty. 11×8, $250.

Baby's First Tooth. 14×9.5, $250.

Life's Greatest Gift. 9×7, $85. *Fan*, $65.

An Armful of Joy. 10×8, $80.

Mothers & Children

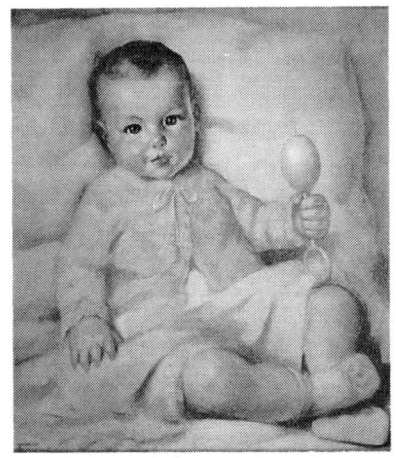

Precious. 12×16, $225. 9" round, $195.

Sitting Pretty. 8×7, $45.

Mother's Joy. 5×3, $195. 8×6, $250.

Among the Daisies. 7×10, $265. 3×2.5, $175. *Book Cover "Little Lassies", 1912*, $125.

Mothers & Children 33

Ring Around Rosy. 5×7, $225.

Garden of Contentment #1. 16×12, $150. 8.5×6.5, $120.

One Strike. 16.5×9, $285. 9×4.5, $235.

A Safe Companion. 7×10, $225. 6×8, $200.

34 *Mothers & Children*

Warm Friends. 16×11, $185. 14×10, $150. *Puzzle*, $95.

A Noble Protector. 20×16, $325. 12×8, $225.

Untitled #12. 14×11, $325.

A Life Saver. 11×8, $275.

Playmate Guardian. 17×10, $165. 10×8, $125. 9×7, $95. *Thermometer*, $80. *Fan*, $80.

Please Don't Make Us Go to Bed. 8×6.75, $285.

The Barefoot Boy. 16×11, $185. 15×10, $150. *Scrapbook Front & Back Cover*, $125. *Puzzle*, $95.

Faith. 11×8.5, $275.

36   *Mothers & Children*

Me and Rex. 7×10.5, $260.

Prepared. 8.25×11.25, $250. 7.5×10, $225.

The Fish Story. 7×10.5, $260.

You Shan't Go Swimming, So There! 2.75×2, $165.

Dogs

Untitled #15. 4.25×7, $200.

No One at Home. *Postcard*, $75.

Just Out. *Postcard*, $75.

Ready for Anything. 6×8, $200. *Chatter Box Magazine*, 1927, $95. *Postcard*, $75.

Who are You? *Postcard*, $75.

Untitled #18. 4.25×12, $200.

Dogs

Hero of the Alps. 8×6, $200.

Untitled #21. 9.5×7.5, $200.

Holding an Investigation. *Postcard*, $75.

Almost. 8×3.25, $200.

Thrills Afield. 20×16, $165. 9.5×6.5, $100. 8×6, $85. *Puzzle*, $85.

Rover. 5×7.5, $195.

A Reliable Guardian. 16×20, $95. 10×12, $75. 6×8, $65. *Puzzle*, $80.

A Trusty Guardian. 7×9, $185. 6×8, $185.

40 Dogs

An Efficient Guardian. 8×10, $95.

Waiting for Their Master. 10×8, $195. 8×6.5, $175. 2.5×2, $95.

On Guard. 11×8, $200. 6×4, $150.

On the Alert. 8×12, $200.

Vigilance. 11.5×10, $150. 11×8, $125. 9×7, $100. 8×6, $90.

Juleposten I Nordlandet. 12×9, $225.

The Anxious Mother. 8×3.25, $175. 10×4, $195.

In Full Chase. 5.5×8, $285.

42 Dogs

In Full Cry. 9×6, $250.

An Afternoon Call. 12×10, $175.

Pals. 8×6.5, $195.

Hunter's Paradise. 16.5×20.5, $145. 12×16, $120. 10×12, $100. 4×5, $75. *Puzzle*, $80. *Wood Plaque*, $45.

At Your Service. 9×6, $175. *Tin Tray*, $195.

44 *Horses*

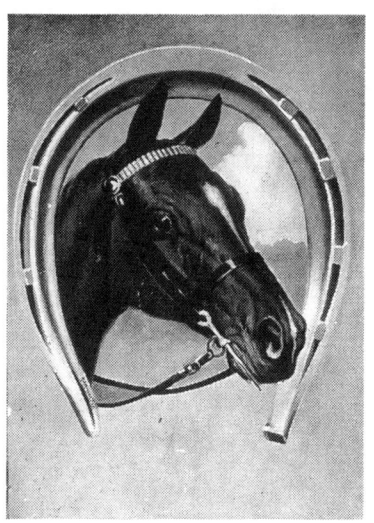

Ready for All Comers. 19×14, $250. 14×11, $200. 12×10, $175.

A Gentle Pair. 12.5×8.5, $200.

Duke. 12×11, $225. 13.5×10.5, $225.

Good Luck. 7×5, $175.

Horses 45

Companion. 10.5×7, $200.

Fraternally Yours. 20×15, $275. 6×4, $145. *Strout Farms Poster*, $185. *Strout Farms Metal Tray*, $125. *T.V. Tray*, $100. *Cover, Strout Farms Magazine*, $95.

Good Morning. 9.5×7.5, $95.

Spick and Span. 12×9, $195. 9×7, $175.

46 *Horses*

Capital and Labor. 10×6, $195. 3×2, $125.

Tom & Jerry. 9×12, $200.

Ready and Willing. 12×8, $200. 10×8, $175. 4×6, $125. 3×3, $95.

At the Fountain. 11×8, $225. 9×7, $195.

Two Old Cronies. 9×12, $200. 7×9, $185.

Friends #2. 21×16, $275. 5.5×7.5, $165.

Horses 47

Pleading at the Bar. 5.5×8, $175.

Bred in the Purple. 16×20, $225. 8×12, $175. 8×5.5, $150.

A Neighborly Call. 14×18, $200. 13×16, $185. 11×14, $165.

Who Said Dinner? 9×12, $225.

Thoroughbreds #2. 12×16, $200. 6×9, $165.

At the End of a Long Day. 5.5×7.5, $185.

48 *Horses*

After the Day's Work. 6×12, $200. 5×11, $185.

Ready for the Day's Work. 5.5×11, $200.

The Day's Work Done. 11×8, $225. 9×7, $195.

A Legal Holiday. 6.5×14, $200. 5×12, $175.

Thoroughbreds #3. 6×8, $175.

Going to the Fire. 13.5×9.5, $295. 9×6.5, $250.

Horses 49

Fording the Stream. 9×5, $225.

Harvesting. 6×8, $195. 5×7, $175. 4.75×5, $150.

The Horse Pasture. 9×12, $195. 4.5×8.5, $175.

Seeking Protection. 10×8, $195. 9×7.5, $175.

Man and Beast Prepare the Land for the Sowing of the Grain. 17×14, $200. 8.75×6, $175.

Untitled #147. 6×8, $165. 5×7, $150. *Ink Blotter*, $95.

50 *Horses*

Well Shod. 8×8, $225.

Old Rose Bud. 16.5×24.5, *on Tin* $450.
Derby Day Poster, 16×24, $275.

Cows 51

U. S. A. Quality. 8×10, $200.

Upland Pastures. 6×4, $175. 3×2, $125. *Puzzle*, $95.

Prize Stock. 8×10, $200. 7.5×11, $190.

The Emperor. 8×6, $225.

Cows

Peaceful Valley #1. 7.25×5.25, $200.

A Proud Mother. 10×8, $200. 8×7, $175.

A Peaceful Summer Day. 9.5×7, $80.

Pasture Stream. 7×11, $195. 5.5×7.5, $165.

Cows 53

Peaceful Valley #2. 8×12, $195.

Untitled #24. 6×4, $195.

A Land of Milk & Honey. 10×7, $175. 6×4, $125. 3×2, $95.

The Edge of the Meadow. 10.5×16, $225. *Postcard*, $75.

In the Pasture Stream. 5×7, $175.

When Evening Calls Them Home. 8×6, $200. 9×7, $175.

Untitled #27. 8×6, $150.

A Shady Pool #1. 20×16, $200. 12×9, $175.

Cows 55

Untitled #30. 22×14, $200.

As the Sun Goes Down. 20×16, $195. 14×11, $150. 12×10, $150. 7×5, $95. *Thermometer*, $85.

Returning From Pasture. 14×10, $200. 13×9, $185. 9×7, $145.

Peace and Contentment. 11×8, $175. 6×5, $125.

When Evening Shadows Fall #1. 9×7, $125. 7×5, $95.

Pride of the Farm #2. 11×9.5, $125. 9.75×7.75, $95. *Puzzle*, $85.

The Close of Day. 8.25×6.25, $200.

A Shady Bower. 12×9, $195.

The Pasture Lane. 15×5, $200.

Future Prize Winners. 7.5×10.5, $225.

Getting Together. 5×15, $225.

The Three Twins. 4×18, $200. 4×10, $185.

Four Chums. 7.75×9.75, $195.

The Watering Place. 5×7, $165. *Postcard*, $75. *Wood Plaque*, $75.

58 Cows

At the Pool. 8×12, $200. 7.5×10, $175.

Contentment. 10×7, $195. 7×5, $175.

A Shady Pool #2. 20×16, $185.
4.5×6.75, $95.

Thoroughbreds #4. 10×16, $200.

A Quiet Country Side. 8×10, $225.

Near Close of Day. 11.5×10, $175.
8×10, $95. *Puzzle*, $85.

Untitled #33. 16×20, $185.

Champions of the West. 8×11, $200.

A Summer Day. 7×10.5, $175. 5.5×7.75, $150.

Peace and Plenty. 8×10, $195. 5×7, $150.

Browsing. 6×8, $200.

Untitled #36. 10×13, $150. 6×8, $95.

Bonnie J. International Champion. 10.5×14, $200. 3.5×5, $150.

Untitled #39. 6×8.5, $185.

Untitled #42. 9×12, $195. 6×8, $125. *Postcard*, $80.

Prides of the West. 8×11, $200.

Untitled #45. 6×8, $195.

The Brook. 5×7, $150. 3.5×5.5, $100. *Postcard*, $75.

Cows 61

Wending Their Way Homeward. 16×20, $195. 9×12, $150. 6×8, $125.

Short Horns. 9.5×13.5, $200. 5.5×10.5, $180. *Puzzle*, $85.

Scotch Shorthorns. 12×16, $200.

Amidst Green Pastures. 9×12, $225. 7×9, $200.

In the Meadow Pasture. 9×12, $195.

A Bunch of Beauties. 8×10, $200.

Cows

Shorthorns Nooning. 11×17.5, $200. 9.5×13.5, $175. 7×10, $150. *Puzzle*, $85.

Untitled #48. 6×8, $185.

Untitled #49. 7×10, $250.

The Herefords #1. 3.5×10, $200.

Where Skies Are Blue. 9×14, $185. 8×12, $165.

Untitled #50. 7×10, $250.

Cows 63

The Herefords #2. 12×16, $200. 8×16, $180. 6×8, $145.

Queen of the Herd. 4.5×7.25, $195.

By Winding Stream. 14×20, $200. 9×6, $150. 7×5, $125. *Postcard*, $85.

Valley Farm. 9×11, $225. 6×8, $200.

In Green Pastures #1. 8×11, $195.

Untitled #57. 8.25×11.5, $195. 6.5×9.5, $175.

Cows

Prize Winners #1. 22×15, $200. 20×12, $185. 3.5×5, $140.

In Pastures Green. 6×6, $195.

An Approaching Storm #1. 8×11, $165.

A Cool Retreat. 8×11, $185. 3.5×7.5, $145.

Country Road. 5×7, $195.

An Approaching Storm #2. *Postcard*, $75.

Cows 65

Prize Winners #2. 9.5×9.75, $175. 7.5×10, $150.

This Good Old Earth. 4×10, $195. The Brook. 5×7, $150. 3.5×5.5, $100. *Postcard*, $75.

A Blue Ribbon Pair. 12×18, $195. 9×13, $175.

Down on the Farm #1. 4.25×6.25, $185.

66 *Feline Family & Bears*

In the Enemy's Country. 17×25, $325. 10.5×14, $200.

Supreme. 9×12, $225.

The Monarch #1. 6×8, $225.

A Royal Outlaw. 6×8, $225. *Puzzle*, $125.

Look Me in the Eye. 5×3, $145.

A Grizzled Old Grizzly. 5×3, $145. *Ink Blotter*, $125.

Monarch of the North #1. 14.5×10, $250.

An Uninvited Guest. 5.5×4, $175.

68 *Feline Family & Bears*

In the Rockies. 14×12, $195.

The Sentry. 16×12, $195. 9×7, $165.
Book Cover *"In the Jungle"*, $95.

High in the Mountains. 20×16, $195.
18×14, $175. 12×10, $150. 8×6, $125.

Eternal Hills. 9×7, $175. 6×4, $150.

Feline Family & Bears 69

The Sentinel. 6×8, $200.

Untitled #60. 12×9, $200. 10×8, $175.

The Silent Rockies. 14×11, $125. 9×7, $85. 7×7, $65. 5×3, $50. *Wood Box Lid*, $75.

Animals - Variety

Untitled #63. 15×5, $200.

Their Journey's End. 15×5, $195. 4.5×1.5, $145.

The Feeding Ground. 15×5, $195. 7.5×2.5, $165.

Northward Bound. 16×11, $200. 12.5×8.5, $185. 10×8, $175.

Animals - Variety 71

When the Day Is Done. 10×6, $95.

The Good Shepherd. 12×20, $175. 12×16, $150. 4.75×8, $95.

Homeward Bound #1. 8×6, $200.

Indian Summer. 18×30, $275. 20×23, $175. 16×20, $145. 14×20, $135. 12×16, $125. 8×10, $100. 6×8, $95.

In Green Pastures #2. 6×8, $200.

A Quiet Pool. 6×8, $175. 6×6, $125.

Animals - Variety

When Shadows Lengthen. 10×8, $150. 7.5×8, $95.

Old Faithful. 13×18, $175. 9.5×7.5, $85.

The Guardian. 8×11, $195.

Watching the Flock. 8×20, $185.

Peaceful Valley #3. 11×8, $175.

Animals - Variety 73

Sunset in the Big North Woods. 10×11, $200.

The Call. 7×10, $200.

The Forest Primeval #1. 8×6, $200.

King of the Silvery Domain. 9.5×7, $125. 7×5, $95. *Fan*, $75. *Thermometer*, $75.

Animals - Variety

A Danger Signal. 14×9, $195. 10×6, $175. 8×6, $165.

The Patriarch. 5×3, $145.

Monarch of the North #2. 15×5, $195. 9×7, $175.

The Monarch #2. 5×3, $145.

Animals - Variety 75

The Night Call. 9×12, $175.

Fury of the Flames. 8×12, $195.

In the Days of Peace and Plenty. 9×12, $175. 6×8, $150.

Battle of the Wild. 19×15, $195. 10×8, $150. 4.5×3.5, $95. *Puzzle*, $85.

The Morning Call. 8×12, $195.

76 *Animals - Variety*

A Brother Elk. 12×10, $250. 5×3, $145.

Evening in the Mountains. 14×10, $175. 11×8, $150.

Forest Fire. 10×8, $195.

Nature's Silvery Retreat. 9.5×7, $150.

Animals - Variety 77

The Forest Primeval #2. 12×10, $175. 11×8, $150.

Over the Top. 12×9, $195. 11×6.25, $175. 8×6, $135.

A Sheltering Bower. 20×16, $165. 20×12, $150. 15×11, $125. 5×4, $75. *Thermometer*, $65.

Good Morning Deer. 12×10, $125. 5×4, $80.

Animals - Variety

Head of the Herd. 5×3, $145.

The Last of the Herd. 10×15, $200. 8.5×12.5, $185.

The Pioneers. 11×19, $200. 10×15, $185.

King of the Clouds. 5×3, $145.

Animals - Variety 79

The Leader. 11×10, $200.

Play While You May. 5×3, $145.

Children of the Forest. 5×3, $145.

Working Overtime. 5×3, $145. *Ink Blotter*, $125.

Gardens

Blue Lake. 18×20, $125. 14×20, $100.

Venetian Garden. 18×30, $285. 12×20, $145. 14×18, $125.

Dreamland. 14×22, $125. 8×12, $75.

Flower Land. 18×30, $250.

Summer's Glory. 19×32, $325. 18×30, $295.

Peace and Sunshine. 21.5×32, $275. 18×30, $250.

Gardens

Garden of Contentment #2. 12.5×20.5, $145. 10×18, $125.

Garden of Happiness #1. 10×18, $145. 9×17, $125.

The Magic Pool. 10×16, $100.

Nature's Grandeur #1. 14×22, $150.

Sapphire Seas. 14×20, $150. 13×17, $125.

Nature's Beauty. 14×28, $165. 14×22, $145. 10×20, $125. *Puzzle*, $85.

Nature's Treasure(s). 18×30, $250. 14×22, $145.

Garden of Love. 10×18, $125. 10×12, $100. 9.5×7, $85. *Thermometer*, $95. *Puzzle*, $75.

Promenade. 14×22, $145. 12×20, $125. 8×12, $75.

Garden of Hope. 14×22, $145. 10×16, $100.

Country Garden. 20×40, $325. 18×30, $250. 14×24, $145.

English Garden. 18×30, $250. 14×20, $95.

Gardens 83

Haven of Beauty. 18×30, $295. 10×18, $145.

Love Birds. 16×13, $150. 10×8, $100. 9×7, $80. *Puzzle*, $85.

Land of Dreams. 16×12, $125. 12×6, $95. 10×8, $85. 9×7, $75. *Puzzle*, $75. *Thermometer*, $75.

Lover's Bower. 9×7, $150. *Fan*, $75.

Gardens

Oh! Rare's the Sunset When Warm O'er the Lakes. 13×10, $150. 12×9, $150. 10×8, $125.

Majestic Splendor. 30×18, $250. 1/2 *Fireplace Screen*, $150.

Untitled #69. 11.5×9, $225.

Rose Bower. 16×10, $100.

Gardens 85

Dreamy Paradise. 16×12, $145. 14.5×10, $125. 9×7, $95. *Puzzle*, $85.

Fountain of Love. 10×15, $100.

Where Memories Stray. 2.75×2.5, $45. *Ink Blotter*, $75.

Moonlight and Roses. 14×18, $145.

In a Lovely Garden Where Dreams Come True. 16×22, $165. 9×12, $125. 7×9, $195. 4×9, $75.

Gardens

Garden of Romance. 22×14, $125. 10×8, $75.

Nature's Retreat. 22×14, $165.

Garden of Happiness #2. 18×14, $145. 16×12, $125. 9.5×7.5, $100.

Midsummer Magic. 22×14, $125. 12×8, $75.

Gardens 87

Garden of Rest. 18×10, $145.

Garden Realm. 20×10, $125.

Blooming Time. 22×16, $175. 18×14, $165. 16×10, $145.

Garden of Nature. 18×10, $145.

Gardens

The Sunny South #1. 16×11, $100. *Fan*, $75.

Nature's Charms. 22×14, $195.

Garden Gate. 22×12, $165. 16×12, $145.

Garden Retreat. 20×10, $100.

Cottages & Rural Landscapes

Home Sweet Home #1. 9×12, $165. 9×7, $95. *Fan*, $75.

An Old-Fashioned Garden. 18×30, $285. 16×22, $185. 14×18, $165.

There's No Place Like Home. 15×20, $195. 10×22, $175. 9×12, $145. 7×9, $125. *Thermometer*, $85.

Down Memory Lane. 10×6, $175. 9×4, $150.

Heart's Desire. 13×27, $200. 14×22, $175. 10×20, $155.

Cottages & Rural Landscapes

The Cottage by the Sea. 12×16, $175. 11×14, $145. *Puzzle*, $85. *Thermometer*, $85.

Wayside House. 30×18, $250. *1/2 Fireplace Screen*, $150.

Where Nature Beats in Perfect Tune. 20×16, $185. 12×9, $145.

Enchanted Steps. 18×14, $165. 20×12, $165.

Cottages & Rural Landscapes 91

It's Only a Cottage / But It's Home. 16×22, $185. 9×12, $155. 7×9, $125. 4×9, $95. *Puzzle*, $95.

A Jersey Homestead. 10×24, $250. 12×16, $225.

Just a Place to Call Our Own. 7×9, $165. 6×8, $145.

Be It Ever So Humble, There's No Place Like Home. 16×22, $175. 9×12, $145. 6×8, $125.

Sweet Ol' Spot. 16×20, $175. 15×19, $175. 9×12, $135.

The Old Home. 16×20, $165.

Cottages & Rural Landscapes

Untitled #72. 20×26, $225. 13.5×16.5, $200.

When the Day Is Over. 10×8, $180. 9×7, $160.

Memories of Childhood Days. 20×16, $175. 12×9, $125.

Home Sweet Home #2. 16×20, $175. 16×22, $175. 9×12, $125. 12.5×12.5, $125. 4×5, $75. *Fan*, $75. *Ink Blotter*, $65.

Cottages & Rural Landscapes

Cottage by the Sea. 12×10, $200.

Rest Haven. 16×10, $185. 8×10, $125. 9×7, $95. 8×6, $85.

Blossom Time. 12×24, $185. 10×20, $165.

Russet Gems. 16×21, $185. 9×12, $130. 4×5, $80. *Puzzle*, $85.

Down on the Farm #2. 8×11, $165.

A Peaceful Day. 8×10, $200. 6×4, $165.

Cottages & Rural Landscapes

Untitled #75. 16×20, $225.

The Old Mill #1. 10×7.5, $125. *Fan*, $85.

Down by the Bridge. 9.5×7, $195. 8×6, $165. 5.5×5, $125. *Thermometer*, $85.

Untitled #77. 12×16, $195. 10×14, $175.

The Old Mill #2. 4.5×6, $165.

Cottages & Rural Landscapes 95

By the Old Mill Stream. 10×8, $135. *Thermometer*, $85. *Fan*, $75.

The Busy Mill. 6×12, $185.

Summertime at Grandpa's. 8×11, $195.

Homeward Bound #2. 8×6, $165. 5.5×3.5, $145.

The Mill and the Birches. 10×8, $175.

Cottages & Rural Landscapes

Untitled #78. 8×20, $225. 8×16, $200.

The Old Well. 5×3, $165.

Peace. 12×18, $195. 9×12, $145. 5×8, $125.

His First Lesson. 9.5×7.5, $250.

Untitled #84. 4×12, $145. 4×10, $135.

Untitled #81. 7×10, $285.

Cottages & Rural Landscapes 97

Dandelion Time. 10×24, $165. 6×14, $95.

Perfect Day. 14×18, $125.

After the Harvest #1. 6×7.5, $175.

Nature's Mirror. 20×32, $250. 18×28, $195.

America's Bread Basket. 16×22.5, $200.

After the Harvest #2. 7×9, $145. 3.5×8, $95.

Rivers & Falls

Valley of Golden Dreams. 14×11, $165. 12×9, $95. 10×7, $75. *Puzzle*, $75.

Untitled #87. 16×10.5, $85. 12×10, $70.

Rocky Waterway. 16×13, $175.

Nature's Sublime Grandeur. 16×20, $125. 9×11.5, $85. 6×8, $65.

Rivers & Falls 99

Heart of the Hills. 10×8, $85. 9×7, $75.

The Majesty of Nature. 8×11, $195.

Bridal Veil Falls - Yosemite. 14×11, $185. 8×6, $125.

Golden West. 13×15, $175. 10×8, $75.

100 *Rivers & Falls*

The Colorful Rockies. 10×8, $85. *Fan*, $65.

Clear Creek Canyon - Colorado. 6×4, $125.

Nature's Sentinels. 11×8, $145.

Sunrise #2. 12×8, $145.

Rivers & Falls 101

The Royal Gorge - Colorado. 9×16, $150. 6×12, $125. 6×4, $85.

Solitary Heights. 8×6, $145.

Lookout Mountain. 5.5×3.5, $95.

The Approaching Storm. 20×16, $100. 12×9.5, $75.

102 *Rivers & Falls*

Moonlight on the Camp #1. 10×8, $150. *Puzzle*, $85. *Fan*, $75.

Columbia River - Oregon. 14×28, $200. 14×20, $175.

Pure and Healthful. 7.5×10.5, $165.

The Winding River. 2×3.5, $65. *Ink Blotter*, $95.

Canadian Landscape. 14×22, $145. 6×14, $65.

Rivers & Falls 103

Untitled #90. 16×10, $95.

The Snow-Capped Mountain. 17×14, $145. 10×8, $95. 7.5×5.5, $75. 8.75×2.75, $45. *Puzzle*, $85. *Fan*, $75. *Wood Plaque*, $55.

Untitled #93. 16×10, $95.

The Natural Bridge of Virginia. 6×4, $75. 3.5×2.5, $35. *Ink Blotter*, $65. *Postcard*, $45.

Rivers & Falls

In America's Wonderland. 22×16, $145. 12×10, $95. 10×8, $75.

Untitled #96. 12×22, $195.

On the Way to the Mill. 11×6.5, $195. 6×9, $125.

Untitled #99. 15×28, $195. 12×24, $145.

Colorado Canyon. 3×2.5, $65. *Ink Blotter*, $95.

Pike's Peak. 5.5×3.5, $95.

Heart of the Seilkerts. 11×8, $145. 8×6, $125. 6×4, $100. *Ink Blotter*, $75.

Mountain Vista. 10×7, $150.

Giant Steps Falls, B.C. 12×9, $95. 11×8.5, $85.

106 *Rivers & Falls*

A Shrine of Nature. 14×11, $165.

Untitled #102. 10×7.5, $145.

Bridal Veil Falls. 3×2.5, $75. *Ink Blotter*, $95.

Vernal Falls - Yosemite, California. 6×4, $95. 3×2.5, $75. *Ink Blotter*, $95.

Rivers & Falls 107

Lower Falls - Yellowstone Park. 5.5×5.5, $95.

Minnehaha Falls. 6×4, $85. 2.5×3, $65. *Ink Blotter*, $85.

Great Fall of Yellowstone. 12×8, $95.

The Bridal Veil Falls of Yosemite Valley. 12×8, $125. 9×7, $100. 6×3, $75. *Postcard*, $75.

108 *Rivers & Falls*

Wonders of Nature. 8×10, $185. *Ink Blotter*, $80.

Yosemite Falls. 5.5×3.5, $95.

Vernal Falls. 11×8, $145.

Untitled #105. 9×13, $195.

Rivers & Falls

Crystal Falls. 2.75×3.5, $75. *Ink Blotter*, $95.

Niagara Falls. 6×4, $95. 2.75×2.5, $65. *Ink Blotter*, $95.

The Artist Supreme. 14×9, $165. 10×8, $145. 10×6, $125.

In the Heart of the Sierra Nevadas. 16×11, $165. 15×10, $145. 9×7, $100.

Rivers & Falls

The Mountain in All Its Glory. 10.5×7, $145.

Sentinel of the Ages. 16×11, $125. 11×8.5, $95.

By a Waterfall. 16×13, $145. 10×7, $75. 7×5, $50. *Puzzle*, $75. *Wood Box Lid*, $75.

Mountains & Lakes

Tourist Mecca. 10×8, $125. 9×7, $100.

In the Land of the Sky. 12×10, $125. 10×8, $95. 8×6, $85. *Fan*, $75.

Mt. Sir Donald. 3×2.5, $65. *Ink Blotter*, $95.

Mt. Rainier #1. 16×20, $185. 10×12, $125. 6×8, $95.

112 *Mountains & Lakes*

Neath Turquoise Skies. 9×7, $95.

In Flanders Field. 10×16, $145. 8×16, $125. 6×12, $95.

The Canyon. 9×7, $165.

Mount Sir Donald - Canada. 16×10.5, $175. 6×4, $95.

Grand Canyon. 5.5×3.5, $95.

Mountains & Lakes 113

Colbourne Buttes - Colorado. 6×4, $95.

The Mountain Trail. 21×16, $195.
14×11, $150.

Where Giants Wrought. 17×12.5, $165.
6×4, $95.

Majestic Solitude. 16×20, $175. 9×12,
$125.

Mountains & Lakes

Untitled #106. 8×12, $175.

The Gateway to Golden Gorge. 10×8, $85. 10×7, $75. 10×5, $65. 5×3, $45. *Fan*, $75.

Sunset Rock (Lookout Mountain). 6×4, $85. 2.75×2.25, $45. *Ink Blotter*, $75. *Postcard*, $75.

Land of Sky Blue Waters. 20×16, $225. 12×9, $165. 8×5.25, $145. *Fan*, $75.

Mountains & Lakes

A Golden Sunset. 9.5×7, $125. 8×7, $95.

Where Peace Abides #1. 10×7, $95. 6.25×4.75, $75.

Birch Bordered Waters. 16×10, $165. 10×7, $95.

A Mountain Paradise #1. 8×15, $95.

Glorious Vista. 18×30, $195. 16×20, $95. 13×15, $85.

116 *Mountains & Lakes*

Purple Majesty. 9×14, $185. 8×12, $125. 7×11, $100.

Lake Louise in the Canadian Rockies. 8.25×6.75, $85. 6×4, $75. 3.75×2.5, $45. *Ink Blotter*, $75.

Nature's Grandeur #2. 6×8, $95.

When Evening Shadows Fall #2. 3×2.5, $45. *Ink Blotter*, $75.

Untitled #108. 6×4, $95.

Mountains & Lakes 117

October Days. 12×9, $125. 9.5×7, $95. 8×6, $75.

The Home of the West Wind. 16×23, $200. 14×23, $195. 7.25×10, $145.

Inspiration Inlet. 18×24, $125. 10.5×20.5, $80.

A Mountain Paradise #2. 16×8.5, $165. 10×7.5, $125.

118 *Mountains & Lakes*

Lake Louise - Alberta. 11×14, $175.

The Rosy Glow of the Land of Promise. 22×16, $195. 13×10, $125. 10×8, $95. 8×6, $85. *Ink Blotter*, $75.

Mount Rainier #2. 16×10.5, $185. 9×7, $110. 8×6, $95. 6×4, $85.

At the Foot Hills of Pike's Peak. 13×10, $125. 10×8, $95. 9×7, $85.

Mountains & Lakes 119

Rocky Mountain Grandeur. 9.5×7, $95.

Untitled #111. 11×14, $175.

Mountain Lake. 20×40, $285.

Among the Snow Capped Peaks of the Rockies. 9×12, $145. 7×9, $125.

Untitled #114. 13×30, $195. 14×28, $185.

120 *Mountains & Lakes*

Land Where Shamrock Grows. 14×22, $165. 18×20, $165. 14×20, $145.

Twilight Glories. 9.5×8, $95. *Fan*, $75.

Where Peace Abides #2. 9×7, $85. 5.75×3.75, $65.

Glacier Nat'l Park. 5.5×3.5, $95.

Mountains & Lakes 121

Mirror Lake. 5.5×5, $95.

Untitled #117. 11×8, $125. 10×7.5, $95.

Mount Shasta. 5.5×3.5, $95.

Mount Shasta - California. 6×4, $95.
3×2.5, $65.

122 *Mountains & Lakes*

Head of the Canyon. 10×13, $165.

Guardian of the Valley. 10×15, $95. 9×12, $75. 8×11, $65. 6×8, $55. 6×4.25, $50. *Puzzle*, $80.

Grand Canyon - America's Wonderland. 16×22, $200. 9×12, $150. *Puzzle*, $95.

A Glimpse of the Colorado. 9.5×14, $165.

Going to Sun Mountain. 7×5, $75. 6×4, $65. 2.75×2.25, $35. *Ink Blotter*, $60.

Mountains & Lakes 123

Mount of the Holy Cross - Colorado. 6×3.5, $95. 3.5×5.5, $65. *Ink Blotter*, $75. *Postcard*, $75.

Untitled #120. 10×7, $125.

Mid Mountain Verdure. 8×6, $145.

A Mountain Lake. 16×20, $165. 9.5×12, $125.

Mt. Rainier Glowing in Rosy Splendor. 13×16, $165. 9×12, $125. 6×9, $95.

124 *Mountains & Lakes*

Mount Rainier #3. 16×11, $145. 6×4, $85. *Postcard*, $75.

Mount Rainier #4. 5.5×3.5, $95.

Untitled #123 (Golden Glow Series). 16×10, $125. 12×9, $75.

In God's Wonderland. 13×10, $195. 10×8, $145. 8.75×4.75, $95. 6.5×3.5, $75.

Mountains & Lakes 125

An Old Oak. 10×16, $160. 9.5×15.5, $145.

A Fairy-Like Vision: Mount Shasta in the Sky. 16×22, $225. 8.5×10.5, $185. 4.75×8.5, $145.

Mount Hood. 16×20, $185. 9×12, $125. 6×8, $75.

Mountain Valley. 10×15, $95.

Nature's Hidden Places. 11.25×8.75, $175. 10×8, $165. *Fan*, $85.

126 *Mountains & Lakes*

The Witching Hour. 16×10, $175.

A Song of Evening. 16×10, $95. *Ink Blotter*, $75.

The Dells of Wisconsin. 5.5×3.5, $95.

Untitled #126. 9.5×15.5, $95.

Mountains & Lakes 127

Sundown on the Marsh. 16×10, $145.

Morning Mists. 16×10, $145.

A Silvery Pathway. 9×6, $165.

Geyser. 20×14, $185. 16×12, $145. 11×8, $125. 11×5, $95. *Travel Magazine Back Cover*, $100.

128 *Roads & Pathways*

Autumn Glow. 18×40, $200.

Pike's Peak From Garden of the Gods. 18×25, $200.

Sunland. 14×26, $165. 14×22, $125.

Autumn Gold. 10×20, $95. 10×18, $85.

Shower of Daises. 10×24, $165. 6×14, $55.

Stately Sentinels. 14×22, $125.

Roads & Pathways 129

Path to the Valley. 16×10, $95.

Untitled #129. 18×13.5, $110. 16×10.5, $95.

An Inviting Pathway. 26×17, $165. 20×14, $145. 16×12, $125. 15×10, $110. 3×2.5, $45. *Ink Blotter*, $75.

The Snow-Capped Peaks. 11×8, $145.

Mountain Glow. 8×7, $145. 6×5, $100.

The Magic Forest. 16×12, $165. 12×9, $125. 9×7, $95.

The Mediterranean Coast. 22×14, $185.

The Good Luck Line. 10×16, $95.

Roads & Pathways 131

Perspective. 18×14, $110. 16×10, $95. 3×2.5, $45. *Ink Blotter*, $75.

The Path to Home. 6×8, $165.

Untitled #132. 16×10, $95.

Untitled #135. 10×8, $145. 9×7, $125.

132 *Roads & Pathways*

Ruins of Ticonderoga. 9×11, $175. 6×7.5, $145.

Oaks by the Roadside. 10.5×16, $95.

Spring Beauties. 10×24, $165. 6×14, $55.

The Mount of the Holy Cross. 20×16, $175. 17×14, $145.

The Glories of Autumn. 10×24, $195. 10×22, $175.

Roads & Pathways 133

Sunset. 10×13, $95. 8×16, $95.

Where Brooks Send Up a Cheerful Tune. 20×16, $195. 14×11, $145. 12×9, $125. 8×16, $125.

Popocatapel - Mexico. 6×4, $95.

The Road of Poplars. 8×16, $75.

Roads & Pathways

After the Storm. 11×16, $85. 9.5×15, $75. 10×12, $65.

A Rustic Bridge. 10×16, $95. *Tray*, $95.

Pike's Peak - Colorado. 6×4, $95.

The Mystic Hour. 11×8.5, $185. 7×5, $145.

Ships & Seascapes 135

Good Ship Adventure. 20×17, $150. 16×10, $125. 12×9, $95. 8.5×7, $75. 6.75×5, $65. *Playing Card*, $25.

Spirit of Adventure. 9.5×7, $125. 9×4, $75.

The Port of Heart's Desire. 15×11, $145. 12×9, $95. *Puzzle*, $85. *Fan*, $75.

Vikings Bold. 4×7.5, $165. 6.75×4.5, $85. *Cover to Tablet*, $75.

136 *Ships & Seascapes*

Off Treasure Island. 9×7, $125. 7.5×5, $80.

River of Romance. 8×14, $145. 5×7, $95. *Puzzle*, $80.

Clipper Ship. 14×18, $75.

Old Ironsides. 9.5×13, $145. 8×12, $125.

Sunset in Normandy. 16×21, $275.

Ships & Seascapes 137

The Treasure Fleet. 9×12, $125. 8×11, $95. 6×10, $85. 4.25×7.75, $75.

The Stairway. 10×7.5, $165. 6.5×4.75, $145. *Fan*, $85.

The Sunny South #2. 18×14, $145. 16×12, $125. 10×8, $95.

In New York Bay. 6×4, $125. *Ink Blotter*, $85.

138 *Ships & Seascapes*

The Heights of Quebec. 10×5, $145. 6×4, $125. *Ink Blotter*, $75.

Palisades of the Hudson. 5.5×3.5, $95.

Kap Nome, Alaska. 8×11, $175. 3.75×5.75, $125.

Cool & Refreshing. 7.5×10.5, $175.

Sunrise, Coast of Maine. 7.5×10.5, $175. 4×6, $125.

Ships & Seascapes

Moonbeam Enchantment. 9×7, $145. 8×6, $135.

Thousand Islands. 5.5×3.5, $95.

Where Dreams Come True. 16×10, $165. 9×7, $125.

A New England Coast. 3×2.5, $125.

The Golden Gate at San Francisco. 7×5, $125. 6×4, $95. 3.5×2.5, $45. *Ink Blotter*, $75.

Hunting & Fishing 141

The Three Pals. 9×12, $185. 7×9, $135.

Their Attack Conquered. 9×12, $195. 6×8, $175.

Good Day's Sport. 8×11, $200.

A Tense Moment. 13×6, $195. 7.75×3.5, $165.

Well Done. 5×8, $185.

Hunting & Fishing

Come Along My Beauty. 6×8, $185. 5×3, $155.

A Thrill Before Breakfast. 11×8.5, $225. 8.5×6, $195.

Fisherman's Luck. 15×5, $200. 12.5×4.75, $185. 7.5×2.5, $165.

Untitled #66. 10×8, $165. *Puzzle*, $265.

Going After the Big Ones. 7.5×5.5, $195.

144 *Western*

The Roundup. 10×8, $165. 8×6, $125.

His Last Cartridge. 10×8, $165. 8×6, $125.

The Forest Ranger. 9×7, $175.

William F. Cody. 13×10, $250. 9×6, $200. 3×2.5, $150.

Oh Susanna - The Covered Wagon. 8×12, $250. 5.5×8, $200.

Western 145

Through the Mountain Pass. 10×8, $225.

First Tourists Visit Old Faithful. 15×9, $250.

The Right Of Way. 22×17.5, $175. 6×8, $165.

Washburn - Langford Expedition Discovers Old Faithful. 15×9, $200.

146 *Western*

By the Campfire Glow. 15×5, $95.

Moonlight on the Camp #2. 10×8, $95.

The Covered Wagon Crossing the Platte River. 9.5×13.5, $225. 8×10, $200. 5×7, $185.

Mount Lefroy. 4×3.5, $165. *Ink Blotter*, $85.

Journey's End - Oregon. 16×22, $250. 10×14, $200.

Native American 147

White Feather. 20×16, $550. 16×12, $375. 15×11, $350.

In Meditation Fancy Free. 24.5×19.5, $450. 14×11, $375. 8×6, $225. *Fan*, $175.

Daughter of the Setting Sun. 20×16, $375. 16×14, $295. 14×11, $265. *Puzzle*, $150.

Flower of the Forest. 16×10, $125. 22×18, $145. 9×7, $95.

148 *Native American*

In Moonlight Blue. 8×6, $165. 7×5, $135.

Untitled #168. 10×7.5, $150.

Daughters of the Incas. 15×11, $375. 9×7, $295.

The Skyline. 9×7, $295.

Good Guide. 12.5×7, $225. 8×6, $175.

Indian Paradise. 12×16, $175. 6.25×8.25, $145. 5×7, $135. *Lid of Box*, $135. *Plaque*, $95.

Edge of Grand Canyon. 8×10, $295.

Untitled #171. 8×6, $175.

150 *Native American*

The Buffalo Hunt. 8×10, $175. 6×8, $125. *Postcard*, $75.

Old Faithful by Moonlight. 15×9, $250.

In the Days of '49. 7×11, $295. 6×8, $250.

Military & Presidents

General "Mad" Anthony Wayne at the Battle of Stoney Point. 9×12, $225.

The Turn of the Tide - Americans at Chateau Thierry. 8×11, $225.

Surrender of Cornwall at Yorktown. 7×9, $195.

Shouting the Battle Cry of Freedom. 22×16, $250.

Tramp, Tramp, Tramp the Boys are Marching. 16.5×12.5, $275.

152 Military & Presidents

Washington at Valley Forge #1.
9.5×12.5, $250. 8×12, $225.

Washington at Valley Forge #2. 5×3.5, $165.

First Raising of the Stars and Stripes at Valley Forge. 8×12, $185. 8×10, $165.

Taking a Trench. 16×20, $275.

Generals Foch, Pershing and Haig Reviewing Their Victorious Troops. 16×20, $275. 9.25×12.5, $195.

Military & Presidents 153

Untitled #141. *Candy Box*, $275.

Supremacy. 16×20, $200.

Untitled #138. 10×5, $195. *Candy Box*, $275.

Untitled #144. 9.5×7.5, $150. 8×6, $125.

154 Military & Presidents

Departure of Columbus. 9×12.5, $195.

Discovery of the Mississippi, 1541. 16×22, $225. 12×20, $200. 12×16, $185. 11×14, $165.

The Political Argument. 7.5×10.5, $225. 5×7, $185. *Postcard*, $75.

Andrew Carnegie. 8×5, $165. *Ink Blotter*, $125.

Grover Cleveland. 5×3.5, $165.

Military & Presidents 155

Abraham Lincoln. 14×10, $200. 12×10, $195. 11×8, $150.

Portrait of George Washington. 22×18, $200. 8×5, $95. *Fan*, $75.

156 *Planes & Trains & Miscellaneous*

The New Overland Express. 9×12, $195. 9×7, $175. *Fan*, $85.

Aces All. 10×8, $250.

An Ambassador of Good Will. 16×22, $225. 10×8, $145. 9×7, $135. 6.5×4.5, $95. *Thermometer*, $125.

The Lone Eagle. 12×16, $225. 6×8, $195.

Planes & Trains & Miscellaneous 157

Out of the Sky He Comes. 7.5×10.5, $250.

Mount Lindbergh. 16×10, $25. 9×7, $15.

A Fallen Monarch. 16×20, $185. 10×13, $95.

Spirit of Discovery. 7.5×10, $250.

The Iron Horse - Driving the Golden Spike. 18.5×24.5, $295.

Between Two Fires. 7×10, $225.

158 *Planes & Trains & Miscellaneous*

Chicago, Milwaukee, St. Paul and Pacific #1. 8×10, $175.

Chicago, Milwaukee, St. Paul and Pacific #2. 8×10, $175.

Chicago, Milwaukee, St. Paul and Pacific #3. 8×10, $175.

Chicago, Milwaukee, St. Paul and Pacific #4. 8×10, $175.

Chicago, Milwaukee, St. Paul and Pacific #5. 8×10, $175.

Chicago, Milwaukee, St. Paul and Pacific #6. 8×10, $175.

Planes & Trains & Miscellaneous 159

Chicago, Milwaukee, St. Paul and Pacific #7. 8×10, $175.

Chicago, Milwaukee, St. Paul and Pacific #8. 8×10, $175.

Chicago, Milwaukee, St. Paul and Pacific #9. 8×10, $175.

Chicago, Milwaukee, St. Paul and Pacific #10. 8×10, $175.

Chicago, Milwaukee, St. Paul and Pacific #11. 8×10, $175.

Chicago, Milwaukee, St. Paul and Pacific #12. 8×10, $175.

160 *Planes & Trains & Miscellaneous*

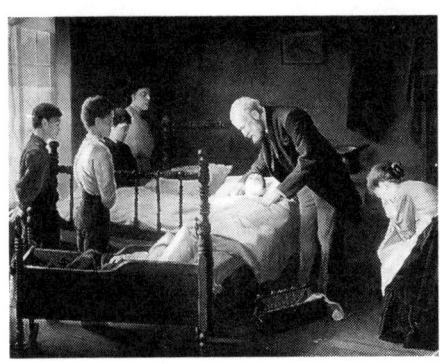

Family Picnic. 7×9, $195. *Puzzle*, $165.

Mother's Day. 9×7, $225.

Untitled #148. 16×20, $225. 13×17, $200.

Down On Grandpa's Farm. 11×7.5, $225. 9×6, $195.

Repairing of All Kinds. 13×10, $285.

Planes & Trains & Miscellaneous 161

Gosh! 8×6, $275.

Poppies. 18×30, $250. 15×20, $145. 12×20, $125.

Faithful and True #1. 7.5×5.5, $265.

Flight to Egypt. 14×10, $245. 8.5×7, $195. *Fan*, $145.

Fox Pseudonyms

Fox pseudonyms are sought after just as avidly as pieces signed by his legal name. Some speculate that he used other names because he was not happy with his work or the publisher wanted to use different artist names for a collection of Fox's work.

Decedents of the Fox family and painting records from print and calendar companies have verified that the other signatures in this chapter are that of R.A. Fox's. There are other artworks that resemble the style in which Fox painted and are signed by other names than what is listed below. Those names however, have not been proven and would only confuse the matter further by including them here.

Following is the list of proven Fox pseudonyms as found in this chapter:

1. J.H. Banks
2. G. Blanchard Carr or B. Carr
3. John Colvin or J. Colvin
4. Arthur DeForest or DeForest
5. Dupre
6. Elmer Louis
7. Musson; H. Musson; Ed. Musson or Edw. Musson
8. George W. Turner
9. Wainright; Charles Wainright; Chs. Wainright; C.N. Wainright; C. Wainright; C. Wain; F. Wainright; Thos. Wainright or Wainwright
10. George White; Geo. W. White; Geo. White
11. George Wood

L. H. Banks 165

Producing the Finest Dairy Products.
10×12, $85.

166 *G. Blanchard Carr*

Cozy Cottage. 14×10, $85.

The Garden Home. 14×10, $85. 12×9, $65.

The Grandeur of Summer. 10×14, $85.

Haven of Splendor. 10×14, $85. 7.5×14, $65.

Watching. 5×7, $80.

J. Colvin 167

Chums. 20×16, $300.

Playmates. 16×11, $225. 12×9, $185.

The Guardian. 14.5×10.75, $285.

On Guard. 13×16, $225. 6×4.5, $150.

A Faithful Guardian. 9×12, $175. 6×9, $145.

Faithful. 10×8, $145.

Untitled #153. 13.5×10.5, $225.

Childhood Days. 9×4, $200.

J. Colvin 169

Their First Lesson. 10×11, $185.

Untitled #150. 8×6, $165.

Their Great Day. *Fan*, $125.

Disputed Property. 7×11, $250.

Close Friends. 11×9, $150. 10×8, $150.

DeForest

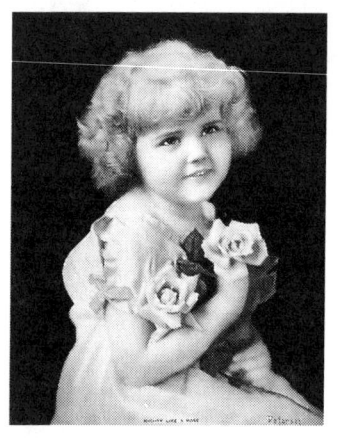

Mighty Like a Rose. 10×8, $85. 8×6, $75.

Curly Locks. 9.5×6.5, $100.

Age of Innocence. 7×5, $100.

Childhood Days. 10×8, $145.

Playmates. 10×8, $100. 8×6, $85.

Speak Rover. 9×7, $145.

A Bounty From Heaven. 8×6, $125.

Strickly Confidential. 10×8, $165. 8×6, $125.

A Barrel of Fun. 10×8, $95.

Esmeralda. 9×7, $165. 8×6, $140.

The Children's Hour. 8×6, $135.

Mother's Darling. 8×6, $100.

Meditation. 10×8, $95.

Pride of the Blue Ridge. 9.5×7, $145.

On Treasure Isle. 9×7, $145.

The Adventuress. 13.5×11, $195. 9.5×7, $165.

A Perfect Melody. 9.5×7, $175.

Mutual Surprise. 10×8, $75.

As Twilight Approaches. 10×8, $85.

A Golden Spot. 12×10, $85. 10×7, $75. 6×4, $65.

Dupre

Aloya of the South Seas. 9.5×7, $165.

In the Land of the Sky Blue Waters. 10×8, $100.

The Chieftain's Pride. 16.5×9, $135. 10×8, $100.

Wanetah. 10×8, $125.

Dupre

At Peace With the World. 9.5×7, $125. 6.5×4.5, $100.

Grandeur of Nature. 10×8, $75. 8×6, $65. 7×6, $45.

By the Zuider Zee. 9.5×7, $75. 8×6, $65.

Elmer Louis 177

Untamed Monarchs. 9×11, $225.

Safe and Secure. 16×20, $245. 10×12, $200. 9×12, $200.

Old Ocean Roars - The Jungle Answers. 12×18, $200. 9×12, $175. *Puzzle*, $85.

Strength and Security. 15×22, $285.

A Royal Pair. 22×17, $285. 12×8, $225.

178 *Elmer Louis*

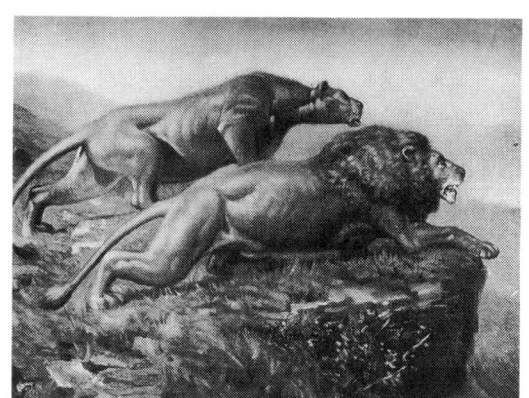

Master of All He Surveys. 8×10, $200.

Ever Watchful. 9.5×11, $200.

Untitled #159. 10×13.5, $245. 7×9, $185.

The Guardian. 16×22, $285. 14×10, $200.

Monarch of All He Surveys. 7.5×5.5, $185. *Candy Box*, $150.

Untitled #156. 12×10, $225. 6×4.25, $145.

Security. 16×20, $285. 9.5×12, $200.

On a Trail. 7×9, $200. 6×8, $185.

Discretion Is the Better Part of Valor. 10×16, $225. 6×9, $145.

Safely Guarded. 16×20, $265. 12×12, $195.

A Critical Moment. 6×8, $165.

Elmer Louis

A Battle Royal. 8×12, $165.

On the Lookout. 14×21, $245. 10×16, $225.

Washington at Headquarters. 10×11, $185. 6×8, $145.

On Rocky Heights. 9×5, $165.

Washington at the Battle of Monmouth. 19×16, $185. 12×9, $175. 8×6, $145.

Elmer Louis 181

The Lure of the Lake. 10×13.5, $150.

Silent Night. 10×13.5, $145.

The Grip of Winter. 10×3, $125.

Musson

A Thoroughbred. 10×16, $125. 8×12, $100. 4.75×6.75, $75.

Untitled #162. 3.5×5.5, $145.

Under the Maples. 5×7, $165.

Four of a Kind. 7.75×5.75, $165.

When the Cows Come Home. 8×6.5, $175.

The Farm Yard. 7×5, $165.

George W. Turner

Off New England Shores. 10×8, $85.

Silvery Divide. 9.75×7.75, $65. 8×6, $45.

C. Wainright

The Flavor of Fall. 10×14, $125. 9.5×12, $100.

The Old Pathway. 13×8, $125. 9.5×6.5, $100.

Nature's White Mantle. 9×7, $45.

Two Medieine River Falls, Montana. 10×8, $45.

C. Wainright 185

Sentinels of the Pass. 10×8, $45.

Paradise. 12×9, $65. 8×6, $45.

At Sundown in the Golden West.
9.5×7, $65. 8×3.5, $45.

A View Through the Timber. 9×6, $100.

Overlooking Emerald Bay. 10×8, $95.

Under the Greenwood Tree. 9.5×12, $125. 6×9, $100.

The Camper's. 12×6, $125. 16×4.5, $95.

The Echoing Call. 10×8, $75.

C. Wainright 187

A Garden of Flowers. 17×9.5, $75. 9.5×7, $65. *Fan*, $45.

Untitled #165. 7×11, $100.

100% Pure; Also, Down on the Farm. 8.5×10.5, $125.

The House by the Side of the Road. 16.5×9, $75. 9.5×7, $65.

C. Wainright

The Old Fishing Hole. 10×8, $100. 8×6, $85.

Paradise Valley. 12×9, $65. 8×6, $45.

The Favorite. 7×5, $175.

Maid in U.S.A. 8×6, $150.

C. Wainright 189

Being Helpful. 8×6, $225.

Quiet Solitude. 8×14, $145.

Washington & LaFayette at Valley Forge. 9×7, $165. *Fan*, $125.

George White

Scenting the Trail. 10×8, $55.

On the Trail. 8×8, $50.

All Set; Also, Hunter's Friend. 9.5×8, $65. 8×6, $45.

At the Foot of Mt. Rainier. 10×8, $65.

Silvery Wonderland. 10×8, $85.

Silvery Grandeur. 10×8, $50. 6.75×4, $40.

The Sentinel of the Night. 10×12, $65. 6×8, $45.

192 George White

The Sweetest Flower That Grows. 10×8, $145.

The Girl of the Golden West. 8×6, $80.

G. *Wood* 193

By a Falling Crystal Stream. 12×10, $65.

W. M. Thompson Introduction

Over the years, prints and calendars by William Thompson have been frequently seen at antique shops and shows across the nation. Many know the artist by one of his various signatures -- W.M. Thompson, W. Thompson, WMT, or just Thompson. Early works show the signature Will Thompson.

Thompson's increasingly popular works have often been confused with those of R. Atkinson Fox. In fact, many people mistakenly believe that Fox and Thompson are the same person. Thompson's daughter, Dorothy Schwalje, graciously offers the following information about her beloved father.

William McMurray Thompson was born in Philadelphia on May 17, 1893. His artistic talent began to show while he was still in grade school. When he was a young boy, the family moved from Philadelphia to Perth Amboy, New Jersey, where his mother died. When his father remarried, life for young Thompson became unhappy, for his stepmother was unloving and abusive. He ran away from home, probably in 1907 or 1908, and gravitated to the New York City art community.

In New York Thompson worked as an apprentice to William Henry Chandler, beginning as a clean-up boy in Chandler's studio and eventually buying the business. He lived in New York on and off until the onset of World War I and his enlistment in the infantry.

After his return from military service, Thompson married Jean Burnett Drysdale in Perth Amboy on May 24, 1919. The couple resided in that city until 1923, when they and their firstborn moved to a new home in Meterchew, New Jersey. Thompson continued to work in his New York studio, despite chronic eye problems caused by mustard gas during the war.

Thompson's favorite works were done on sketching trips to such places as the lakes and pastures of Vermont, the shorelines of Massachusetts and New Jersey, and the fields, lanes, and woods close to home. His last sketches were done on a trip to Lake Louise, Banff National Park, and the Monterey

Peninsula. He usually sketched in oils on an 8-by-10 inch canvas board; afterward, in his studio, he copied the sketches to larger stretched canvases of various sizes. Many times, pencil and pad were all Thompson used to record a pleasing landscape. In later years he used a camera.

As a commercial artist, Thompson preferred pastels because of their reproductive qualities. Pastels were also quick to make, which enabled him to speedily process orders for greeting card companies and large lithography firms.

During the Great Depression, orders began to dwindle, which forced Thompson to close his New York studio and open one in an upstairs room of his house. But his financial struggles continued; his work came to a virtual standstill. To support his wife and four children, Thompson sought employment with the U.S. government. Once he became acclimated to his new job, he never again worked as a commercial artist. Instead, he served as superintendent of the New Jersey Home for Disabled Veterans until his retirement in 1954. He continued to paint during these years, but only for his own pleasure and that of friends.

Thompson shared with his family the beauty he saw not only in visual art, but also in literature, music, and nature. His daughter remembers him as intelligent, compassionate, gentle, and although not a churchgoer, deeply religious. He adored his children, always encouraging them in their life pursuits, and took enthusiastic pride in their accomplishments. His advice to them was simple: "If you want to paint, first you must draw." And the quote that always brought a smile to his face was "Curved is the line of beauty."

Thompson's marriage was friendly, caring, and comfortable. His wife encouraged and praised him without fail, particularly during the Depression. Because Thompson was terribly modest about the caliber of his work, his wife worked hard to build his confidence and motivation.

In the mid-1950s Thompson's wife died of lung cancer, and shortly thereafter he was diagnosed with Parkinson's disease. The onset of this disease and its symptomatic tremors made it impossible for him to produce the high-quality work he demanded of himself. This was a sad time in his life, as he was unable to artistically express himself in the way he wanted.

In 1966, a fire erupted during the night in the house Thompson shared with his daughter and her family. Thompson's son-in-law, after successfully evacuating his wife and children, lost his life while saving Thompson. The physical and emotional stress of these events worsened Thompson's physical condition, and he died nine months later, on July 29, 1967, in Edison, New Jersey.

During his short but prolific career as a commercial artist, Thompson was widely admired for his renderings of such scenes as Western landscapes, snow-covered countryside, and moonlit campfires. Prints of his pastels, with their subtle blends of colors, are still eagerly sought after today.

Moonlight

Evening. 9.5×7.5, $35.

Autumn Moonlight. 12×16, $45.

Midst Snow and Ice. 14×17, $50. 6×8, $25.

The Old Home. 9.5×7.5, $35.

198 *Moonlight*

Bright as Day. 16×20, $55.

How Dear to My Heart #1. 13×10, $45.

The Mountaineer's Home. 9.25×7.25, $35.

How Dear to My Heart #2. 10×13, $45.

Moonlight 199

The Dearest Spot on Earth. 9.5×7.5, $55.

When Shadows Fall. 9.5×7, $35.

Home Is Where the Heart Is. 9×7, $35.

Peaceful Valley. 6.75×5, $20.

Moonlight

Untitled #2. 4×3, $15.

The Day's Long Labor Ends. 8×6, $25.

Silver Moon. 6×4, $40.

Breaking Clouds. 6×8, $25.

By the Light of the Silvery Moon. 9.5×7.5, $35.

Moonlight 201

My Old Kentucky Home. 8.75×7, $35.

Moonbeam Reflections. 12×10, $40.

Summer Night. 9×11, $45. 6×8, $25.

Rural Landscapes

Untitled #4. 9.5×7.5, $35.

In the Gloaming. 10×8, $40. *Puzzle*, $25.

Eventide. 9.5×7.25, $35. 7.5×5, $25.

End of the Trail. 7×5, $20.

Rural Landscapes

The Setting Sun. *Puzzle*, $45.

Memory Lane #1. 9×7, $35.

Autumn's Golden Fleece. 20×15, $55. 8×6, $25. 4.5×3.5, $20. 3.5×2.5, $15.

Untitled #6. 8×10, $40. 6.5×8.5, $35. *Ink Blotter*, $25.

In the Shock. 8×10, $60.

204 *Rural Landscapes*

Memory Lane #2. 10×8, $40.

Apple Blossom Time. 9.5×6.75, $55.

Untitled #8. 12×9, $45.

Wayside Scenes. 9.5×7.5, $35.

Rural Landscapes 205

Rural Sunset. 12×9, $45.

Sunset. 9.5×7.5, $55.

At the End of the Road. 10.25×7.75, $40.

Ever Flowing, Ever Turning. 8×6, $25. *Puzzle*, $20.

206 Rural Landscapes

The Abandoned Mill. 7.75×10.25, $40.

A Frosty Morning. 6×8, $25.

Showering Autumn Leaves. 4×9, $30.

Where the Silver Waters Flow. 7.75×9.75, $40.

Rural Landscapes 207

Sunset Ridge. 12×9, $45. 8×6, $25.   Untitled #10. 12×10, $45.

208 *Mountains & Other Landscapes*

Lake O'Hara. *Puzzle in Box,* 12×9, $50. *Puzzle* 16×12, $25.

Untitled #12. 6×8, $25.

A Mountain Paradise.

Nature's Blue and Gold. 9×12, $45.

Mountains & Other Landscapes 209

Lake Louise. 16×22, $55. 9×12, $35. 6×8, $25.

Still Waters. 11.5×4.25, $25.

Cradled in Mountain Beauty. 15.5×11.5, $50. 12×9, $40. 8×6, $25.

Spring Time in the Rockies. 9.5×7, $35. 7×5, $20.

210 *Mountains & Other Landscapes*

The Glory of the West. 9.75×6.75, $40. 7×5, $15.

Silvery Moonlight Charms. 9.5×7, $35.

Moonlight Reflections #1; Also titled, Moonlight on the Rockies. 9×7, $45. 7×5, $20.

Paradise Valley. 9.5×7.5, $45. 8×6, $25.

Mountains & Other Landscapes 211

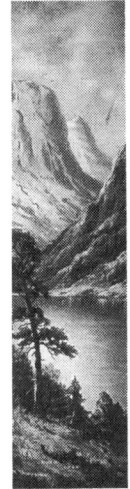

Land of the Contented Heart. 10×2.5, $55.

The Gateway of Glory. 9.5×7.5, $40.

Autumn Brilliance. 8×6, $25. 7×5, $20.

Woodland Splendor. 8×10, $40.

Mountains & Other Landscapes

Golden Boughs. 10×2.5, $55.

Haunt of the Moose. 12×9, $45.

Untitled #16. 12×9, $45. 11×8, $40. 8×6, $25.

Great Outdoors. 9×11, $45. 7×9, $35.

Mountains & Other Landscapes 213

Flying Low. 6×8, $25.

On the Wing. 12×16, $55. 9×12, $45.
Thermometer, $55.

Untitled #18. 10.5×14.5, $45.

214 *Rivers & Falls*

Restless Waters. 9×6.75, $35.

Holy Cross Mountains. 6.75×5, $20.

Rushing Waters. 9.5×7, $35.

Sportsmen's Paradise. 9×7, $35.

Rivers & Falls 215

A Mountain Vista. 7.75×3.5, $45. 12×9, $40.

Twin Falls. 7×5, $20.

By a Waterfall. 14.5×9.5, $50. 12×9, $45. 11×7, $40. 10×5, $30.

God's Handiwork. 13×2.75, $55.

Rivers & Falls

Untitled #26. 9×7, $35.

Monarchs of the Golden West. 9×7, $35.

Untitled #28. 16×12, $50. 8×6, $25.

Moonlit Waters. 9×7, $55. 9.5×6.5, $55.

Rivers & Falls 217

Gliding Over Boulders. 13×4, $30.

Untitled #22. 7×5, $25.

Untitled #24. 16×12, $50.

Untitled #20. 16×12, $50.

218 Rivers & Falls

The Waterfall. 16×12, $50. 12×9, $40.
Puzzle, $75. *Ink Blotter*, $10.

Untitled #30. 12×9, $45.

Sunset in the Mountains; Also titled, Golden Waterway. 16×12, $50. 11×8, $40. 9×7, $35.

Untitled #32. 16×12, $50. 12×9, $45.

By a Mountain Stream. 16×11.75, $50. 9×7, $35. 8×6, $25. *Thermometer*, $35.

220 *Campfires*

Song of the Mountain. 9.25×7, $35. 8×6, $25. *Ink Blotter*, $25.

Untitled #34. 12×9, $50. 12×9, $40. 7×6, $25.

Lakeside Camp. 15×11.5, $50. 11×8.5, $40. 9.75×7.75, $35.

Silver Moon and Amber Stream. 8×10, $40. 2.75×3.5, $15. *Puzzle*, $25.

Campfires 221

Deep in the Woody Wilderness. 22×16, $60. 12×10, $45.

Pine Camp. 7.75×5.75, $25.

Untitled #36. 12×16, $50. 9×12, $45. 6×8, $25.

222 Cottages & Gardens

Memories Garden #1. 4×7, $65.

Untitled #38. 7.5×5.5, $65.

Home & Flower's. 8.25×7, $35.

Untitled #40. 12×9, $50.

Cottages & Gardens 223

Untitled #44. 8×6, $40.

Washington's Birthplace - Virginia.
9.75×7.75, $55.

Untitled #46. 8×10, $50.

Untitled #42. 8×12, $50.

Memories Garden #2. 9.25×6.75, $45.

Cottages & Gardens

Cottage Neath the Moon. 10×8, $50.

A Breath of Spring. 4×5, $25.

Grandmother's Cottage. 12×16, $65. 9×12, $50. *Puzzle*, $75.

Untitled #48. 9×7, $40.

A Spring Morning. 6×8, $30.

By Placid Lake and Winding Road. 7×5, $30.

Untitled #50. 16×20, $80.

A Cozy Cottage. 9×12, $65.

Land of Dreams, Pasadena, Cal.. 16×20, $80.

226 *Snow Scenes*

When Winter Rules. 5.75×7.75, $25. 4×6, $20.

Wintry Night. 20×14, $50.

Untitled #54. 12×9, $45.

Untitled #52. 8×6, $25.

Snow Scenes

Untitled #56. 12×9, $45.

When Winter Comes Again. 6×8, $25.

Silent Winter Night. 6×8, $25.

Untitled #58. 8×6, $25.

Snow Scenes

Winter Nightfall; Also titled, In Winter's Ermine Robe. 6×8, $25.

Untitled #60. 12×9, $45. 8×6, $25.

Winter Trail to Home. 10×8, $40. 8×6, $25. 7×5, $20.

A Golden Glow of Welcome. 9.5×7, $35. *Thermometer*, $35.

Snow Scenes 229

Untitled #62. 8×6, $25.

Wane of Winter Day. 10×8, $35. 8×6, $25. *Puzzle*, $25.

Cabin in the Hills. 9×7, $35. 6.75×4.75, $20.

Winters Crimson Sunset. 16×12, $50. 8×6, $25.

230 Snow Scenes

Snow Scene. 9.25×6.75, $35.

Golden Light of Peace. 12.5×10, $45. 8×6.75, $25.

Silvery Pathway. 9×7, $35.

Winters Silberkleid; Also titled, Winters Silver and Gold. 13×6.5, $45. 9×7, $35.

Snow Scenes 231

The Road to Home. 9.25×6.75, $55.

Untitled #66. 14×18, $50.

Untitled #64. 5×7, $20.

Road to Home; Also titled, When Winter Comes. 14×10, $55. 14×10, $45. 6.75×5, $20.

232 *Snow Scenes*

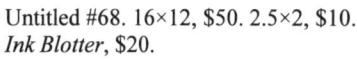

Untitled #68. 16×12, $50. 2.5×2, $10. *Ink Blotter*, $20.

In Winter's Embrace. 9.5×7.5, $40. 7.75×5.75, $25.

The Snow Is Newly Laid. 4×9.75, $35.

Winter Moonlight #1. 9×6.5, $45.

Snow Scenes 233

Mid Winter Night. 9.5×7.5, $35.

Untitled #72. 6×8, $25.

Winter Sunset. 9×7, $35.

Untitled #74. 12×16, $50.

Snow Scenes

Untitled #76. 8×10, $40.

Cozy Cabin. 7.75×10.25, $40.

Christmas Eve in the Mountains. 10×8, $40.

Winter Splendor. 9.75×7.75, $50.

A Winter Evening. 12×16, $50. 8×10, $40.

Winter Moonlight #2. 7×5, $20.

Where Shelter Awaits. 9.25×6.75, $35.

A Glow of Welcome. 9.5×4.5, $30.

236 Snow Scenes

Sunset's Mellow Glow. 9.25×6.75, $50.

The Cheering Welcome Glows. 9.75×7.75, $35.

Untitled #78. 12×9, $45.

Twas the Night Before Christmas. 9×12, $50.

Snow Scenes 237

Untitled #80. 8×10, $40.

Untitled #82. 10×7.5, $50.

238 *Ships & Sea*

The Lighthouse. 5.75×7.75, $25.

Homeward Bound. 6×4, $20.

In Full Sail. 6×8, $25.

A Moonlight Melody. 10×12, $45.

In the Land of Hearts Desire. 5.75×7.75, $45.

Moonlight Reflections #2. 10×8, $40.

The Land of Loveliness. 15×2.75, $50.

Where the Sun Sinks Down at the Close of Day. 14×18, $50. 10×12, $45.

A Tropical Moon. 5.75×7.75, $25.

Rocky Shore. 8×9.75, $40. 6×8, $25.

240 Ships & Sea

Midsummer Night. 10.75×8.5, $40.

Tropical Splendor. 9.75×7.75, $40.

Sunset Glow. 7×9.5, $40.

Tropical Moonlight. 10×7.5, $40. 5.5×4, $20.

Index

Fox

Symbols

100% Pure 187

A

A Barrel of Fun 172
A Battle Royal 180
A Blue Ribbon Pair 65
A Bounty From Heaven 171
A Brother Elk 76
A Bunch of Beauties 61
A Cool Retreat 64
A Critical Moment 179
A Danger Signal 74
A Fair Guide 16
A Fair Skipper 17
A Fairy-Like Vision: Mount Shasta in the Sky 125
A Faithful Guardian 168
A Fallen Monarch 157
A Garden of Flowers 187
A Gentle Pair 44
A Glimpse of the Colorado 122
A Golden Spot 174
A Golden Sunset 115
A Grizzled Old Grizzly 67
A Jersey Homestead 91
A Land of Milk & Honey 53
A Legal Holiday 48
A Life Saver 34
A Loya of the South Seas 175
A Mountain Lake 123
A Mountain Paradise #1 115
A Mountain Paradise #2 117
A Neighborly Call 47
A New England Coast 139
A Noble Protector 34
A Peaceful Day 93
A Peaceful Summer Day 52
A Perfect Melody 174
A Proud Mother 52
A Quiet Country Side 58
A Quiet Pool 71
A Reliable Guardian 39
A Royal Outlaw 66
A Royal Pair 177
A Rustic Bridge 134
A Safe Companion 33
A Shady Bower 56
A Shady Pool #1 54
A Shady Pool #2 58
A Sheltering Bower 77
A Shrine of Nature 106
A Silvery Pathway 127
A Song of Evening 126
A Summer Day 59
A Tense Moment 141
A Thoroughbred 182
A Thrill Before Breakfast 142
A Treat 28
A Trusty Guardian 39
A View Through the Timber 185
Abraham Lincoln 155
Aces All 156
The Adventuress 23, 173
After a Days Work 48
After the Harvest #1 97
After the Harvest #2 97

After the Storm 134
Age of Innocence 170
All Set 190
Almost 38
America's Bread Basket 97
Amidst Green Pastures 61
Among the Daisies 32
Among the Snow Capped Peaks of the Rockies 119
An Afternoon Call 42
An Ambassador of Good Will 156
An Approaching Storm #1 64
An Approaching Storm #2 64
An Armful of Joy 31
An Efficient Guardian 40
An Inviting Pathway 129
An Old Oak 125
An Old-Fashioned Garden 89
An Uninvited Guest 67
Andrew Carnegie 154
The Anxious Mother 41
The Approaching Storm 101
The Artist Supreme 109
As the Sun Goes Down 55
As Twilight Approaches 174
At Peace With the World 176
At Sun Down in the Golden West 185
At the End of a Long Day 47
At the Foot Hills of Pike's Peak 118
At the Foot of Mt. Rainier 191
At the Fountain 46
At the Pool 58
At Your Service 43
Autumn Glow 128
Autumn Gold 128

B

Baby's First Tooth 31
The Barefoot Boy 35
Battle of the Wild 75
Be It Ever So Humble, There's No Place Like Home 91
Beauties of the Country 17
Being Helpful 189
The Best Piemaker in Town 18
Between Two Fires 157

Birch Bordered Waters 115
Blooming Time 87
Blossom Time 93
Blue Lake 80
Bluegrass Beauties 27
Bonnie J. International Champion 60
Bred in the Purple 47
The Bridal Veil Falls of Yosemite Valley 107
Bridal Veil Falls 106
Bridal Veil Falls - Yosemite 99
The Brook 60
Browsing 59
The Buffalo Hunt 150
The Busy Mill 95
By a Falling Crystal Stream 193
By a Waterfall 110
By the Camp Fire Glow 146
By the Old Mill Stream 95
By the Zuider Zee 176
By Winding Stream 63

C

The Call 73
The Camper's 186
Canadian Landscape 102
The Canyon 112
Capital and Labor 46
Carefree 18
Champions of the West 59
Chicago, Milwaukee, St. Paul and Pacific #1 158
Chicago, Milwaukee, St. Paul and Pacific #2 158
Chicago, Milwaukee, St. Paul and Pacific #3 158
Chicago, Milwaukee, St. Paul and Pacific #4 158
Chicago, Milwaukee, St. Paul and Pacific #5 158
Chicago, Milwaukee, St. Paul and Pacific #6 158
Chicago, Milwaukee, St. Paul and Pacific #7 159
Chicago, Milwaukee, St. Paul and Pacific #8 159

Chicago, Milwaukee, St.
    Paul and Pacific #9
    159
Chicago, Milwaukee, St.
    Paul and Pacific #10
    159
Chicago, Milwaukee, St.
    Paul and Pacific #11
    159
Chicago, Milwaukee, St.
    Paul and Pacific #12
    159
Chieftains Pride 175
Childhood Days 168, 170
Children of the Forest 79
The Children's Hour 172
Chrysanthemums 16
Chums 167
Clear Creek Canyon -
    Colorado 100
Cleopatra 23
Clipper Ship 136
The Close of Day 56
Close Friends 169
Colbourne Buttes -
    Colorado 113
Colorado Canyon 104
The Colorful Rockies 100
Columbia River - Oregon
    102
Come Along My Beauty
    142
Companion 45
Contentment 58
Cool & Refreshing 138
The Cottage by the Sea 90
Cottage by the Sea 93
Country Garden 82
Country Road 64
The Covered Wagon
    Crossing the Platte
    River 146
Cozy Cottage 166
Crystal Falls 109
Curly Locks 170

D

Dandelion Time 97
Daughter of the Setting
    Sun 147
Daughters of the Incas
    148
Dawn 19
Day Dreams #1 19
Day Dreams #2 20
The Day's Work Done 48
Deering 25
The Dells of Wisconsin
    126

Departure of Columbus
    154
Discovery of the
    Mississippi, 1541
    154
Discretion Is the Better
    Part of Valor 179
Disputed Property 169
Down by the Bridge 94
Down Memory Lane 89
Down on Grandpa's Farm
    160
Down on the Farm #1 65
Down on the Farm #2 93
Dream Castle 22
Dream Land 80
Dreamy Paradise 85
Duke 44

E

The Echoing Call 186
Edge of Grand Canyon
    149
The Edge of the Meadow
    53
Elysian Fields 19
The Emperor 51
Enchanted Steps 90
English Garden 82
Esmeralda 172
Eternal Hills 68
Evening in the Mountains
    76
Ever Watchful 178

F

Faith 35
Faithful and True #1 161
Faithful and True #2 25
Faithful 168
Family Picnic 160
The Farm Yard 182
Fascinating 15
The Favorite 188
The Feeding Ground 70
First Raising of the Stars
    and Strips at Valley
    Forge 152
First Tourists Visit Old
    Faithful 145
The Fish Story 36
Fisherman's Luck 142
The Flavor of Fall 184
Flight to Egypt 161
Flower Land 80
Flower of the Forest 147
Fooling Him 28
Fording the Stream 49

244 *Index*

The Forest Primeval #1 73
The Forest Primeval #2 77
The Forest Ranger 144
Forest Fire 76
Fountain of Love 85
Four Chums 57
Four of a Kind 182
Fraternally Yours 45
Friends #1 27
Friends #2 46
Fury of the Flames 75
Future Prize Winners 57

G

Garden Gate 88
The Garden Home 166
Garden of Contentment #1 33
Garden of Contentment #2 81
Garden of Happiness #1 81
Garden of Happiness #2 86
Garden of Hope 82
Garden of Love 82
Garden of Nature 87
Garden of Rest 87
Garden of Romance 86
Garden Realm 87
Garden Retreat 88
The Gates of Dream Land 22
The Gateway to Golden Gorge 114
General Foch, Pershing and Haig Reviewing Their Vitorious Troops 152
General "Mad" Anthony Wayne at the Battle of Stony 151
Getting Together 57
Geyser 127
Giant Steps Falls, B.C. 105
The Girl of the Golden West 192
The Girl of the Golden West #1 29
The Girl of the Golden West #2 30
Glacier Nat'l Park 120
The Glories of Autumn 132
Glorious Vista 115
Glory of Youth 15
Going After the Big Ones 143
Going to Sun Mountain 122
Going to the Fire 48
The Golden Gate at San Francisco 140

Golden West 99
The Good Shepherd 71
Good Day's Sport 141
Good Guide 149
Good Luck 44
The Good Luck Line 130
Good Morning 45
Good Morning Deer 77
Good Ship Adventure 135
Gosh! 161
Grand Canyon - America's Wonderland 122
Grand Canyon 112
The Grandeur of Summer 166
Grandeur of Nature 176
Great Fall of Yellowstone 107
The Grip of Winter 181
Grover Cleveland 154
The Guardian 72, 167, 178
Guardian of the Valley 122

H

Harvesting 49
Haven of Beauty 83
Haven of Splendor 166
Head of the Canyon 122
Head of the Herd 78
Heart of the Hills 99
Heart of the Selikerts 105
Hearts Desire 89
The Heights of Quebec 138
Her Pet 26
The Herefords #1 62
The Herefords #2 63
Hero of the Alps 38
High in the Mountains 68
His First Lesson 96
His Last Cartirdge 144
Holding an Investigation 38
The Home of the West Wind 117
Home Sweet Home #1 89
Home Sweet Home #2 92
Homeward Bound #1 71
Homeward Bound #2 95
The Horse Pasture 49
The House by the Side of the Road 187
Hunter's Paradise 42

I

In a Lovely Garden Where Dreams Come True 85
In America's Wonderland 104
In Flanders Field 112

In Full Chase 41
In Full Cry 42
In God's Wonderland 124
In Green Pastures #1 63
In Green Pastures #2 71
In Meditation Fancy Free 147
In Moonlight Blue 148
In My Garden of Dreams 24
In New York Bay 137
In Pastures Green 64
In the Days of '49 150
In the Days of Peace and Plenty 75
In the Enemy's Country 66
In the Heart of the Sierra Nevadas 109
In the Land of the Sky 111
In the Land of the Sky Blue Waters 175
In the Meadow Pasture 61
In the North Woods 29
In the Pasture Stream 54
In the Rockies 68
In the Valley of Enchantment 19
Indian Paradise 149
Indian Summer 71
Inspiration Inlet 117
The Iron Horse - Driving the Golden Spike 157
It's Only a Cottage / But It's Home 91

J

Jealousy 25
Journey's End - Oregon 146
Juleposten I Nordlandet 41
June Morn 22
Just a Place to Call Our Own 91
Just Out 37

K

Kap Nome, Alaska 138
King of the Clouds 78
King of the Silvery Domain 73

L

Lake Louise - Alberta 118
Lake Louise in the Canadian Rockies 116
Land of Dreams 83
Land of Sky Blue Waters 114
Land Where Shamrock Grows 120
The Last of the Herd 78
The Leader 79
Life's Greatest Gift 31
The Lone Eagle 156
Look Me in the Eye 67
Look Pretty 31
Lookout Mountain 101
Love Birds 83
Lover's Bower 83
Love's Paradise 20
Lower Falls - Yellowstone Park 107
The Lure of the Lake 181

M

The Magic Forest 130
The Magic Pool 81
Maid in U.S.A. 188
Majestic Solitude 113
Majestic Splendor 84
The Majesty of Nature 99
Man and Beast Prepare the Land for the Sowing of the Grain 49
Master of All He Surveys 178
Maud Muller 17
Me and Rex 36
Meditation 173
Meditation #1 15
Meditation #2 21
The Mediterranean Coast 130
Memories of Childhood Days 92
Mid Flowers Fair 17
Mid Mountain Verdure 123
Midsummer Magic 86
Mighty Like a Rose 170
The Mill and the Birches 95
Minnehaha Falls 107
Mirror Lake 121
The Monarch #1 66
The Monarch #2 74
Monarch of All He Surveys 178
Monarch of the North #1 67
Monarch of the North #2 74
Moonbeam Enchantment 139
Moonlight and Roses 85
Moonlight on the Camp #1 102
Moonlight on the Camp #2 146
The Morning Call 75
Morning Mists 127
Mother's Darling 172
Mother's Day 160
Mother's Joy 32
The Mount of the Holy Cross 132

Mount of the Holy Cross - Colorado 123
Mount Hood 125
Mount Lefroy 146
Mount Lindbergh 157
Mount Rainier #1 111
Mount Rainier #2 118
Mount Rainier #3 124
Mount Rainier #4 124
Mount Rainier Glowing in Rosy Splendor 123
Mount Shasta 121
Mount Shasta - California 121
Mount Sir Donald 111
Mount Sir Donald - Canada 112
The Mountain in All Its Glory 110
Mountain Glow 130
Mountain Lake 119
The Mountain Trail 113
Mountain Valley 125
Mountain Vista 105
Music of the Waters 21
Mutual Surprise 174
My Castle of Dreams 20
My Pet 29
The Mystic Hour 134

N

The Natural Bridge of Virginia 103
Nature's Beauty 81
Nature's Charms 88
Nature's Grandeur #1 81
Nature's Grandeur #2 116
Nature's Hidden Places 125
Nature's Mirror 97
Nature's Retreat 86
Nature's Sentinels 100
Nature's Silvery Retreat 76
Nature's Sublime Grandeur 98
Nature's Treasure(s) 82
Nature's White Mantle 184
Near Close of Day 58
Neath Turquoise Skies 112
The New Overland Express 156
Niagara Falls 109
The Night Call 75
No One at Home 37
Northward Bound 70

O

O... 25
Oaks by the Roadside 132
October Days 117

Off New England Shores 183
Off Treasure Island 136
Oh Susanna - The Covered Wagon 144
Oh! Rare's the Sunset When Warm O'er the Lakes 84
Old Faithful 72
Old Faithful by Moonlight 150
The Old Fishing Hole 188
The Old Home 91
Old Ironside 136
The Old Mill #1 94
The Old Mill #2 94
Old Ocean Roars - The Jungle Answers 177
Old Pals 26
The Old Pathway 184
Old Rose Bud 50
The Old Well 96
On a Trail 179
On Guard 40, 167
On Rocky Heights 180
On the Alert 40
On the Lookout 180
On the Trail 190
On the Way to the Mill 104
On Treasure Isle 173
One Strike 33
Oriental Beauties 23
Oriental Dreams 19
Out of the Sky He Comes 157
Over the Top 77
Overlooking Emerald Bay 186

P

Palisades of the Hudson 138
Pals 42
Paradise 185
Paradise Valley 188
The Pasture Lane 57
Pasture Stream 57
The Path to Home 131
Path to the Valley 129
The Patriarch 74
Peace 96
Peace and Contentment 55
Peace and Plenty 59
Peace and Sunshine 80
Peaceful Valley #1 52
Peaceful Valley #2 53
Peaceful Valley #3 72
Perfect Day 97
Perspective 131

Pike's Peak 105
Pike's Peak - Colorado 134
Pike's Peak From Garden of
   the Gods 128
The Pioneers 78
Play While You May 79
Playmate Guardian 35
Playmates 167, 171
Pleading at the Bar 47
Please Don't Make Us Go to
   Bed 35
The Political Argument 154
Popocatepetl - Mexico 133
Poppies 161
The Port of Heart's Desire 135
Portait of George Washington
   155
Precious 32
Prepared 36
Pride of the Blue Ridge 173
Pride of the Farm #1 18
Pride of the Farm #2 56
Prides of the West 60
Prize Stock 51
The Prize Winner 18
Prize Winners #1 64
Prize Winners #2 65
Producing the Finest Dairy
   Products 165
Promenade 82
Pure and Healthful 102
Purple Majesty 116

Q

Queen of the Herd 63
Quiet Solitude 189

R

Ready and Willing 46
Ready for a Cantor 26
Ready for All Comers 44
Ready for Anything 37
Ready for the Days Work 48
Repairing of All Kinds 160
Rest Haven 93
Returning From Pasture 55
The Right Of Way 145
Ring Around Rosy 33
River of Romance 136
The Road of Poplars 133
Rocky Mountain Grandeur
   119
Rocky Waterway 98
Romance Canyon 22
The Rosy Glow of the Land
   of Promise 118
Rose Bower 84
Rose Fair 15

The Roundup 144
Rover 39
The Royal Gorge - Colorado
   101
Ruins of Ticonderoga 132
Russet Gems 93

S

Safe and Secure 177
Safely Guarded 179
Sapphire Seas 81
Scenting the Trail 190
Scotch Shorthorns 61
Security 179
Seeking Protection 49
The Sentinel 69
Sentinel of the Ages 110
The Sentinel of the Night 191
Sentinels of the Pass 185
The Sentry 68
Short Horns 61
Shorthorns Nooning 62
Shouting the Battle Cry of
   Freedom 151
Shower of Daises 128
The Silent Rockies 69
Silent Night 181
Silvery Divide 183
Silvery Grandeur 191
Silvery Wonderland 191
Sitting Pretty 32
The Skyline 148
The Snow Capped Mountain
   103
The Snow-Capped Peaks 129
Solitary Heights 101
Speak Rover 171
Spick and Span 45
Spirit of Adventure 135
Spirit of Discovery 157
Spirit of the Harvest 23
Spirit of Youth 20
Spring Beauties 132
The Stairway 137
Stately Sentinels 128
Strength and Security 177
Strickly Confidential 171
Summer's Glory 80
Summertime at Grandpa's 95
Sundown on the Marsh 127
Sunland 128
The Sunny South #1 88
The Sunny South #2 137
Sunrise #1 21
Sunrise #2 100
Sunrise, Coast of Maine 138
Sunset 133
Sunset Dreams 19

Sunset in Normandy 136
Sunset in the Big North Woods 73
Sunset Rock 114
Supremacy 153
Supreme 66
Surrender of Cornwall at Yorktown 151
Sweet Ol' Spot 91
The Sweetest Flower That Grows 192

T

Taking a Trench 152
Their Attack Conquered 141
Their First Lesson 169
Their Great Day 169
Their Journey's End 70
There's No Place Like Home 89
This Good Old Earth 65
Thoroughbreds #1 28
Thoroughbreds #2 47
Thoroughbreds #3 48
Thoroughbreds #4 58
Thousand Islands 139
Three Friends 29
The Three Pals 141
The Three Twins 57
Thrills a Field 39
Through the Mountain Pass 145
Tom & Jerry 46
Tourist Mecca 111
Tramp, Tramp, Tramp the Boys are Marching 151
The Treasure Fleet 137
The Treat 26
The Turn of the Tide - Americans at Chatea Luthierry 151
Twilight 20
Twilight Glories 120
Two Medieine River Falls, Montana 184
Two Old Cronies 46

U

U.S.A Quality 51
Under the Greenwood Tree 186
Under the Maples 182
Untamed Monarchs 177
Untitled #3 27
Untitled #6 27
Untitled #9 28
Untitled #12 34
Untitled #15 37
Untitled #18 37
Untitled #21 38
Untitled #24 53
Untitled #27 54
Untitled #30 55
Untitled #33 59
Untitled #36 59
Untitled #39 60
Untitled #42 60
Untitled #45 60
Untitled #48 62
Untitled #49 62
Untitled #50 62
Untitled #57 63
Untitled #60 69
Untitled #63 70
Untitled #66 142
Untitled #69 84
Untitled #72 92
Untitled #75 94
Untitled #77 94
Untitled #78 96
Untitled #81 96
Untitled #84 96
Untitled #87 98
Untitled #90 103
Untitled #93 103
Untitled #96 104
Untitled #99 104
Untitled #102 106
Untitled #105 108
Untitled #106 114
Untitled #108 116
Untitled #111 119
Untitled #114 119
Untitled #117 121
Untitled #120 123
Untitled #123 124
Untitled #126 126
Untitled #129 129
Untitled #132 131
Untitled #135 131
Untitled #138 153
Untitled #141 153
Untitled #144 153
Untitled #147 49
Untitled #148 160
Untitled #150 169
Untitled #153 168
Untitled #156 179
Untitled #159 178
Untitled #162 182
Untitled #165 187
Untitled #168 148
Untitled #171 149
Upland Pastures 51

V

The Valley of Enchantment #1 20
The Valley of Enchantment #2 21
Valley Farm 63
Valley of Golden Dreams 98

Venetian Garden 80
Vernal Falls 108
Vernal Falls - Yosemite, California 106
Vigilance 41
Vikings Bold 135
The Village Belle 16

W

Wanetah 175
Waiting for Their Master 40
Warm Friends 34
Washburn - Langford Expedition Discovers Old Faithful 145
Washington at Headquarters 180
Washington at the Battle of Monmouth 180
Washington & LaFayette at Valley Forge 189
Washington at Valley Forge #1 152
Washington at Valley Forge #2 152
Watching the Flock 72
Watching 166
Water Lilies 16
The Watering Place 57
Wayside House 90
Well Done 141
Well Shod 50
Wending Their Way Homeward 61
When Evening Calls Them Home 54
When Evening Shadows Fall #1 56
When Evening Shadows Fall #2 116
When Shadows Lengthen 72
When the Cows Come Home 182
When the Day Is Done 71
When the Day Is Over 92
Where Brooks Send Up a Cheerful Tune 133
Where Dreams Come True 139
Where Giants Wrought 113
Where Memories Stray 85
Where Nature Beats in Perfect Tune 90
Where Peace Abides #1 115
Where Peace Abides #2 120
Where Skies Are Blue 62
White Feather 147
Who are You? 37
Who Said Dinner? 47
William F. Cody 144
The Winding River 102
The Witching Hour 126
Wonders of Nature 108
Working Overtime 79

Y

Yosemite Falls 108
You Shan't Go Swimming So There! 36

Thompson

A

A Breath of Spring 224
A Cozy Cottage 225
A Frosty Morning 206
A Glow of Welcome 235
A Golden Glow of Welcome 228
A Moonlight Melody 238
A Mountain Paradise 208
A Mountain Vista 215
A Spring Morning 225
A Tropical Moon 239
A Winter Evening 235
The Abandoned Mill 206
Apple Blossom Time 204
At the End of the Road 205
Autumn Brilliance 211
Autumn Moonlight 197
Autumn's Golden Fleece 203

B

Breaking Clouds 200
Bright as Day 198
By a Mountain Stream 219
By a Waterfall 215
By Placid Lake and Winding Road 225
By the Light of the Silvery Moon 200

C

Cabin in the Hills 229
The Cheering Welcome Glows 236
Christmas Eve in the Mountains 234
Cottage Neath the Moon 224
Cozy Cabin 234

Cradled in Mountain Beauty 209

D

The Day's Long Labor Ends 200
The Dearest Spot on Earth 199
Deep in the Woody Wilderness 221

E

End of the Trail 202
Evening 197
Eventide 202
Ever Flowing, Ever Turning 205

F

Flying Low 213

G

The Gateway of Glory 211
Gliding Over Boulders 217
The Glory of the West 210
God's Handiwork 215
Golden Boughs 212
Golden Light of Peace 230
Grandmother's Cottage 224
Great Outdoors 212

H

Haunt of the Moose 212
Holy Cross Mountains 214
Home & Flower's 222
Home Is Where the Heart Is 199
Homeward Bound 238
How Dear to My Heart #1 198
How Dear to My Heart #2 198

I

In Full Sail 238
In the Gloaming 202
In the Land of Hearts Desire 238
In the Shock 203
In Winter's Embrace 232

L

Lake Louise 209
Lake O'Hara 208
Lakeside Camp 220
The Land of Loveliness 239
Land of Dreams, Pasadena, Cal. 225
Land of the Contented Heart 211
The Light House 238

M

Memories Garden #1 222

Memories Garden #2 223
Memory Lane #1 203
Memory Lane #2 204
Midst Snow and Ice 197
Midsummer Night 240
Mid Winter Night 233
Monarchs of the Golden West 216
Moonbeam Reflections 201
Moonlight Reflections #1 210
Moonlight Reflections #2 238
Moonlit Waters 216
The Mountaineer's Home 198
My Old Kentucky Home 201

N

Nature's Blue and Gold 208

O

The Old Home 197
On the Wing 213

P

Paradise Valley 210
Peaceful Valley 199
Pine Camp 221

R

Restless Waters 214
The Road to Home 231
Road to Home 231
Rocky Shore 239
Rural Sunset 205
Rushing Waters 214

S

The Setting Sun 203
Showering Autumn Leaves 206
Silent Winter Night 227
Silver Moon and Amber Stream 220
Silver Moon 200
Silvery Moonlight Charms 210
Silvery Pathway 230
The Snow Is Newly Laid 232
Snow Scene 230
Song of the Mountain 220
Sportsmen's Paradise 214
Spring Time in the Rockies 209
Still Waters 209
Summer Night 201
Sunset Glow 240
Sunset in the Mountains 219
Sunset Ridge 207
Sunset 205
Sunset's Mellow Glow 236

T

Tropical Moonlight 240
Tropical Splendor 240
Twas the Night Before Christmas 236
Twin Falls 215

U

Untitled #2 200
Untitled #4 202
Untitled #6 203
Untitled #8 204
Untitled #10 207
Untitled #12 208
Untitled #16 212
Untitled #18 213
Untitled #20 217
Untitled #22 217
Untitled #24 217
Untitled #26 216
Untitled #28 216
Untitled #30 218
Untitled #32 219
Untitled #34 220
Untitled #36 220
Untitled #38 222
Untitled #40 222
Untitled #42 223
Untitled #44 223
Untitled #46 223
Untitled #48 224
Untitled #50 225
Untitled #52 226
Untitled #54 226
Untitled #56 227
Untitled #58 227
Untitled #60 228
Untitled #62 229
Untitled #64 231
Untitled #66 231
Untitled #68 232
Untitled #72 233
Untitled #74 233
Untitled #76 234
Untitled #78 236
Untitled #80 236
Untitled #82 236

W

Wane of Winter Day 229
Washington's Birth Place - Virginia 223
The Waterfall 218
Wayside Scenes 204
When Shadows Fall 199
When Winter Comes Again 227
When Winter Rules 226
Where Shelter Awaits 235
Where the Silver Waters Flow 206
Where the Sun Sinks Down at the Close of Day 239
Winter Moonlight #1 232
Winter Moonlight #2 235
Winter Nightfall 228
Winter Splendor 234
Winter Sunset 233
Winter Trail to Home 228
Winters Crimson Sunset 229
Winters Silberkleid 230
Wintry Night 226
Woodland Splendor 211

About the Author

Patricia Gibson is widely recognized as the leading expert in dealings with the artworks of R. Atkinson Fox and William M. Thompson.

Patricia started collecting Fox and Thompson at the same time, simply because she liked them. With an inheritance from her father's estate, Patricia decided to invest into the artworks, but had no idea how far this commitment would take her.

In the course of her collecting, Patricia acquired duplicates which she began selling. Her reputation as a dealer began to grow along with the demand for the artwork.

Patricia's extensive collection today includes original paintings, prints, calendars, and puzzles. It's the largest collection of its kind in the world.

Patricia buys and sells the works of Fox and Thompson at antique shows, in antique shops and through national antique collecting publications. A highly respected member of the Fox community, she resides in Newark, California.

New Books From Collectors Press

The Best Seller is Now Even Better

This expanded, second edition contains nearly 500 photographs in 275 of the most informative pages available anywhere. You will find every print, every calendar, every poster, illustrated book and magazine known to exist. This indispensable reference is a must for anyone interested in Maxfield Parrish.
$19.95 plus $2.50 shipping.

The Colors Come to Life

For the first time ever, the Edison Mazda images Maxfield Parrish painted for General Electric are available as a separate and distinct body of work. Published with permission of General Electric Company, theses beautiful, oversized books are alive with the rich, luminous colors of Maxfield Parrish.
$17.50 Plus $2.50 Shipping

Send checks to:
Collectors Press • Suite 11B
P.O. Box 230986 • Portland, OR 97281

VISA / MasterCard
CALL (503) 684-3030